DOES YOUR
VOTE COUNT?

DOES YOUR VOTE COUNT?

WRITTEN BY
PAUL KEMP

INTERVIEWS EDITED BY
CRISS HAJEK, MALCOM FRASER

AND JOHN CASSANO

Benson & Hedges

BREAKOUT EDUCATIONAL NETWORK
IN ASSOCIATION WITH
DUNDURN PRESS
TORONTO · OXFORD

Publisher: Inta D. Erwin
Copy-editor: Anne Holloway, First Folio Resource Group
Production Editor: Amanda Stewart, First Folio Resource Group
Designer: Bruna Brunelli, Brunelli Designs
Printer: Webcom

National Library of Canada Cataloguing in Publication Data

Kemp, Paul
    Does your vote count?/by Paul Kemp.

One of the 16 vols. and 14 hours of video which make up the
    underground royal commission report
Includes bibliographical references and index.
ISBN 1-55002-433-7

    1. Democracy—Canada. 2. Canada—Politics and government.
3. Federal government—Canada. I. Title. II. Title: underground royal
commission report. III. Title: A call to account

JL75.K44 2002   320.971   C2002-902313-0

1   2   3   4   5   07   06   05   04   03

Printed and bound in Canada.
Printed on recycled paper. ♻
www.dundurn.com

More extensive transcripts of the interviews contained in this book can be found in *A Call to Account: Empirical Evidence and Reference Guide*, edited by Criss Hajek.

Exclusive Canadian broadcast rights for the *underground royal commission* report

intelligent television

Check your cable or satellite listings for telecast times

Visit the *urc* Web site link at:
www.ichanneltv.com

The *underground royal commission* Report

Since September 11, 2001, there has been an uneasy dialogue among Canadians as we ponder our position in the world, especially vis à vis the United States. Critically and painfully, we are re-examining ourselves and our government. We are even questioning our nation's ability to retain its sovereignty.

The questions we are asking ourselves are not new. Over the last 30 years, and especially in the dreadful period of the early 1990s, leading up to the Quebec referendum of 1995, inquiries and Royal commissions, one after another, studied the state of the country. What *is* new is that eight years ago, a group of citizens looked at this parade of inquiries and commissions and said, "These don't deal with the real issues." They wondered how it was possible for a nation that was so promising and prosperous in the early 60s to end up so confused, divided, and troubled. And they decided that what was needed was a different kind of investigation — driven from the grassroots 'bottom,' and not from the top. Almost as a provocation, this group of people, most of whom were affiliated with the award winning documentary-maker, Stornoway Productions, decided to do it themselves — and so was born the *underground royal commission*!

What began as a television documentary soon evolved into much more. Seven young, novice researchers, hired right out of university, along with a television crew and producer, conducted interviews with people in government, business, the military and in all walks of life, across the country. What they discovered went beyond anything they had expected. The more they learned, the larger the implications grew. The project continued to evolve and has expanded to include a total of 23 researchers over the last several years. The results are the 14 hours of video and 16 books that make up the first interim report of the *underground royal commission*.

So what *are* the issues? The report of the *underground royal commission* clearly shows us that regardless of region, level of government, or political party, we are operating under a wasteful system ubiquitously lacking in accountability. An ever-weakening connection between the electors and the elected means that we are slowly and irrevocably losing our right to know our government. The researchers' experiences demonstrate that it is almost impossible for a member of the public, or in most cases, even for a member of Parliament, to actually trace how our tax dollars are spent. Most disturbing is the fact that our young people have been stuck with a crippling IOU that has effectively hamstrung their future. No wonder, then, that Canada is not poised for reaching its potential in the 21st century.

The *underground royal commission* report, prepared in large part by and for the youth of Canada, provides the hard evidence of the problems you and I may long have suspected. Some of that evidence makes it clear that, as ordinary Canadians, we are every bit as culpable as our politicians — for our failure to demand accountability, for our easy acceptance of government subsidies and services established without proper funding in place, and for the disservice we have done to our young people through the debt we have so blithely passed on to them. But the real purpose of the *underground royal commission* is to ensure that we better understand how government processes work and what role we play in them. Public policy issues must be understandable and accessible to the public if they are ever to be truly addressed and resolved. The *underground royal commission* intends to continue pointing the way for bringing about constructive change in Canada.

— Stornoway Productions

14 hours of videos also available with the *underground royal commission* report. Visit Stornoway Productions at www.stornoway.com for a list of titles.

TABLE OF CONTENTS

PREFACE

We are witnessing institutional change, if not failure, on a very large scale. The power, influence and even relevance of Parliament are under threat. This is serious because Parliament is increasingly failing to hold the government to account.

Donald Savoie,
Governing from the Centre:
The Concentration of Power in Canadian Politics

Parliament. Failure. Accountability. All very serious and important words, but there is no getting around it: words like "accountability" bore the hell out of most people. So does the word "Parliament" for that matter.

Such weighty words aside, I had to keep reminding myself why I was writing this book. The answer, summed up in the quote above, was simple. Like it or not, governments matter greatly to our lives. So does Parliament. And it is accountability that ties them together. We ought to be concerned that the vote we cast every four years is put to use in conducting the affairs of this country, supposedly on our behalf, by the members of Parliament we elect. Clearly each and every one of us has a stake in the performance of our politicians.

From the radio or TV stations we tune into, to the type of wheat used in our morning bagel, to where we buy our books, everything in this country is regulated by the laws Parliament passes on our behalf. The federal government takes $170 billion of taxes from us and Parliament authorizes the expenditure of every last cent. Parliament decides how much money we can put in our RRSPs. It determines what substances in our air are considered toxic, how fat our steaks can be and what airlines we can travel on. It even dictates which satellite TV channels we are permitted (or not permitted) to beam into our homes. One might conclude that government, with the authority of Parliament, has us all in a noose.

But isn't the government us? Aren't we the government? Aren't the MPs we elect supposed to be our eyes and ears on the floor of the House of Commons, fusing all our wishes and desires into action?

When Canadians want a more efficient public health-care system, a bigger or smaller military, tax cuts, the restoration of the death penalty or better security at our airports, we expect the people we elect to echo our will. We count on them to defend our interests, pass our laws and spend our tax money to our benefit. But do they? Do we citizens even know how our government and our Parliament work? I don't think I am going out on a limb to suggest that the answer is a resounding no.

This book will explode any illusions Canadians harbour about their governing institutions, Parliament in particular. Parliament is failing us all and failing us badly. The executive branch of our government — traditionally this meant the Cabinet, but increasingly it means the prime minister — and the central agencies of government (including the top echelons of the civil service) now control Parliament.

The bottom line is that Canadians aren't governing themselves well. Parliament is supposed to be our country's legislature, endowed with the duty to oversee the government — to keep it in check. It is not doing that job any longer. Today the government controls Parliament.

Accountability in government falls far outside the issue of right-wing versus left-wing politics and certainly outside the debate over big government versus small government. This book is not intended to examine or even question how much money our government spends on health care, immigration, airports or the military. It asks, instead, if the money spent or the laws passed by our government do what they are supposed to do. It asks who's checking.

After seven years of investigating accountability in government, I can categorically state that government and democracy in Canada do not work the way Canadians think they do. Our vote counts for little, if anything, anymore. There are those who say that that democracy can never be perfect, and that Canada's parliamentary system of government is the best in the world. There are also those, quoted in the pages of this book, who claim that Canada has the most open and accountable government in the world. My experience contradicts this viewpoint. If it *is* true, then it presents a sad portrait of the rest of the world's democracies.

This book does not rehash the arguments presented in political science textbooks about how government *supposedly* works in this country; instead it portrays how it *actually* works. My challenge was to test and prod our political system to come to an objective and honest conclusion about the predicament of our system of government. I am confident that once you have read this book you will be unnerved by its underlying message. I know I am.

To strengthen my case I purposely worked hard at finding people from all sides of the political arena, people with experience in the government trenches. I asked them tough questions, made them draw on their parliamentary and government experiences, and encouraged them to reflect on the question of whether or not our government acts in accordance with the wishes of its citizens through our elected Parliament. I will let the evidence speak for itself.

My hope is that this book will take readers deep inside the arena of parliamentary politics and show in an offbeat, experiential way how the real game of politics is played in Canada. Why offbeat? Because the way this book is organized is probably unlike any other book you have read.

There are four key points about the contents and style of this book and how it came together.

First, I have not cluttered this book with any graphs, charts or statistical analysis to bolster the points I make. I have presented the evidence that I have personally gathered by going through the videotapes and transcripts of nearly 500 on-camera interviews filmed for a series of television programs, documentaries, university teaching materials and books that all deal with how we Canadians govern ourselves. Some of the TV programs have already been broadcast nationally, while others are still in production. All were filmed over the past seven years, but most were filmed in the past 18 months. All deal with various pressing issues facing our country today, mainly the role of our members of Parliament and our system's accountability to the voters. The text of this book comes exclusively from what people we have interviewed have said to our TV cameras. We have used only *their* words about Parliament and the MP's role.

Our interviewees include former ambassadors; senior civil servants; past and present MPs, Cabinet ministers and senators; former deputy ministers; long-time journalists and authors; lobbyists — and even generals. I hope you will agree that the people I quote are all legitimate and credible spokespeople. They come from varying political persuasions, but each has participated in one way or another, or witnessed first hand, what I believe has been the decline of our Parliament over the past 35 years.

Secondly, although I have personally been involved in conducting nearly 300 on-camera TV interviews during this project, my colleagues conducted the other 200 interviews I have since watched and drawn upon. Dozens of people were involved with our work, but Jay Innes, who is based in Ottawa, and Robert Roy, who is based in Toronto, conducted most of the other 200 interviews. I should add that both Robert and Jay were influential in bringing together many of these interview subjects and in researching and drafting the questions we asked. Both men helped me immensely in how I think about these issues.

Thirdly, although we asked the questions and focused the discussion, the interviewees themselves provided the answers. I wish to thank each and every one for their time in front of our cameras. On average these interviews took 45 minutes to one hour, or longer. Some of our interviewees engaged us in debate, others clearly didn't enjoy our questions; some seemed astounded by the depth of our questions, while others simply said no to our requests for interviews. Prime Minister Jean Chrétien turned down repeated requests to be interviewed, as did former prime ministers John Turner and Brian Mulroney. Former prime minister Joe Clark accepted our invitation. Some Cabinet ministers, such as Pierre Pettigrew and Allan Rock, strung us along for months before ultimately refusing; in contrast, Brian Tobin granted us five interviews during his time in Cabinet.

Perhaps most upsetting, yet not so surprising in our highly politicized system, was that Gordon Osbaldeston, Paul Tellier and Mel Cappe, all former clerks of the Privy Council, and all having served for extensive periods at the highest ranks in Canada's civil service, refused to speak on camera. Their reluctance made me wonder what memories they were uncomfortable sharing, especially in the case of Mr. Osbaldeston and Mr. Tellier, who have long departed from government service. I greatly miss the contribution that their reflective comments and insights on the system would have made to this book. (Mr. Osbaldeston, I should note, was gracious enough to give me an hour of his time at his home in London, Ontario, but asked that none of my notes be used in the production of the television series.)

Jay Innes and I tried valiantly to have current and former members of the Prime Minister's Office (PMO) agree to be interviewed. Prime Minister Chrétien's office shot down our requests repeatedly. I concluded that if you are not part of the media game in Ottawa, you are not on the PMO's radar. If your media and political track records are unknown, it will not deal with you. Former members of the PMO under Brian Mulroney, who are now beyond the reach of power and negative media coverage, were more generous with their time, and their memories offered a candid look at how they think the system works. Overall, most interviewees were friendly, reflective and more than willing to give us their time. Thanks again to all of them.

Finally, the quotes presented here are taken from hundreds of separate interviews, and all of the subjects have their own way of speaking and their own style of responding to our questions. I have tried to edit the interviews to preserve their integrity, intent and context. My only editorial liberty has been to place their comments in an order that best serves to illustrate my overall thesis. None of the interviewees intentionally responds to or backs up any other. I have sequenced their statements (offered as answers to the questions they were asked) thematically and endeavoured to present their points of view as clearly as possible.

The themes and evidence speak for themselves most of the time. I have, however, provided personal anecdotes to set up the story. These insights are mine and mine alone.

Enough said about the process of putting this book together. Now to answer the bigger question: Does Your Vote Count?

Paul Kemp

CHAPTER 1

The MP's Role:

From Responsible Government to Paralysis in Only 30 Years

Canadians like to look at politics through the lens of the pollster, so let's begin by examining a poll. A 1999 United Nations poll stated that only 46 percent of Canadians believe that Parliament represents them, down from over 80 percent in the 1960s. More importantly, most Canadians believe that the government wastes our money. Only 12 percent believe government is efficient.

Another more recent poll was conducted in April of 2002. In this Léger Marketing poll, which reportedly unnerved Prime Minister Chrétien, a staggering 69 percent of Canadians said they believed "corruption" was widespread within the federal government.

Do these numbers surprise you? Anecdotal evidence suggests that people in their 30s and younger have little allegiance to their government institutions. Sure they like "free health care" and RSP tax credits, but most hold government in fairly low regard. As far as Parliament and our elected politicians are concerned, if younger Canadians even think of them at all, they place them right at the bottom of society's totem pole. Why such a precipitous drop in just over 30 years? Clearly the reason goes beyond simply the "declining deference to authority" that people so often cite as the explanation.

Perhaps the real reason is that the public's disregard for Parliament and government is warranted. Perhaps our politicians are not doing the job they are supposed to be doing.

Anyone who has ever tried to tackle these issues knows that exploring the intricacies of Canadian politics is a tricky assignment. There is a profound puzzlement among Canadians about how their government, Parliament and politics operate. As citizens we have built up myths about how things really work. This is understandable: we hit the ballot box only every four years or so, and election time is often the only occasion that we actually see our member of Parliament. What do our politicians do during the time between elections? What is their job? Most Canadians believe that their MP represents them. I would venture that most even believe that their MP has a say in the decision-making process of this country. But what really happens to your vote after it is cast? Does a citizen's vote matter once an MP arrives in Ottawa?

Canadians have a considerable stake in the performance of their members of Parliament, but their MPs' performances are being judged by the wrong criteria, criteria that have changed remarkably from what was traditionally expected of an MP. No two Canadians share the same idea of what an MP should or shouldn't be. Even many MPs seem to be unsure of what their role is.

I have compiled a number of the differing views I heard while interviewing dozens of MPs. In fairness, these quotes are in no way a complete analysis of what each of these individual MPs had to say about the issue, but they do reveal where many of our political problems stem from.

John Nunziata, Liberal MP, 1984–1996; Independent MP 1996–2000

As far as being a representative, I consider it my legal and moral responsibility to represent the people of my riding in Ottawa, not the reverse. My responsibility is not to sell government policy to the riding or to simply be another vote in order to ensure that the government gets its way on every piece of legislation. My view has always been that where the best interests of the riding conflict with the position of the political party, the riding's views should always lead the way.

15

Judy Wasylycia-Leis, New Democratic MP, 1997–Present

I am in politics because I believe government has a role to play in ensuring that the wealth of the nation is shared and that everybody is able to participate in conditions of equality.

I see my job in government as twofold. On the one hand I have to keep fighting for systemic change. I have to fight for the federal government to be involved in housing programs, in social service supports and health initiatives. But at the same time, I have to convince them that those programs won't succeed unless they work hand in hand with communities like Winnipeg North Centre and local organizations.

The other half of the job is to demand that government be involved in the redistribution of wealth so that there is equality between communities and so that places like Winnipeg North Centre are not abandoned and left to fare on their own.

I believe that I can be effective whether I am in government or in opposition. I think half of an MP's role is to empower people who feel helpless and vulnerable and hopeless. If I can give people a voice so that their concerns are recognized and translated into action, I will have done my job. I think for my riding, an NDP voice in Parliament is about the best bang you can get for your buck today.

Scott Brison, Progressive Conservative MP, 1997–Present

One of the most important jobs of a member of Parliament is not just speaking in the House of Commons, but listening in his or her constituency. When I'm in Kings-Hants, I listen. When I'm here in the House of Commons, in either the main chamber or the committee rooms, I speak.

In a well-represented democracy, sometimes you stand in your place and say or do things that perhaps your constituents don't agree with. I've done that a couple of times on issues of principle that I felt strongly about. I'm glad that I was able to do that and that people continued to feel comfortable enough with me and with the quality of representation that I provided to re-elect me. They didn't send a lap dog to Ottawa for the prime minister; they sent a representative to stand up for them.

16

We're not elected only to represent the short-term views of our constituents. As parliamentarians in a representative democracy, we also have to represent the interests of all Canadians. That perspective is commonly referred to as Burkean, after Edmund Burke, the political theorist who once said that a member of Parliament belongs to his constituents during elections and between elections he belongs to his country. You somehow have to find ways to bring your constituents' best interests in line with those of all Canadians.

There is an important line that needs to be respected between representing one's constituents in a fundamentalist, populist way and being an effective member of Parliament. That's why one of my other goals in Parliament is to have more free votes in the House of Commons, which I feel doesn't necessarily contradict my strong political party loyalty.

Brian Tobin, **Former Liberal MP and Cabinet Minister**

The issues in my riding are jobs, health care, regional development and what role Atlantic Canada will have within this country. I have a mandate as a member of Parliament to try and facilitate economic growth and investment in my own riding and my own province. Clearly I'm going to make sure that my area is well represented, and clearly I'm going to make sure that my constituency has a fair opportunity to participate in the kind of programming the government offers. I bring forward proposals from my constituents and from private sector players, from communities, from economic development groups, tourism development groups within my riding and the folks at Atlantic Canada Opportunities Agency. But I wouldn't want to suggest that because I am the minister of industry there's going to be a special allocation for my riding as opposed to other ridings.

I prefer not to talk about what members of Parliament can do versus what ministers of industry can do. That's an unfair way to characterize the role of MPs. I've been on both sides of the House, and I like to think that I made a contribution on both sides of the House of Commons.

Deborah Grey, **Reform and Canadian Alliance MP, 1989–Present**

People have sent me to Ottawa four times now. People know I'm not just going to disappear; they know I'm going to go there, stand up and go after those guys and hold them accountable. That has been my role so far as a member of the opposition: to hold government accountable. I point out their weaknesses and attempt to show a constructive alternative, illustrating some of the things that we will do when we form government.

People recognize me because they watch me on TV, on Question Period. They know that I'm not going to horse around. I don't have time to waste giving them a line. Doing that has never served anyone well in life and I just cannot play games.

I have constituency hours, at my office, where my constituents come in with federal issues, the Canada Pension Plan disability benefits being a huge one that we deal with. The whole thing is just a nightmare and really needs to be revamped. Even Liberals are frustrated with it, so dealing with this goes beyond partisanship. Other things that we deal with are immigration cases, for example, people trying to have a family reunification. There are also income tax problems, Revenue Canada, and Human Resources Development issues. People get letters in the mail from Revenue Canada or the Immigration Department, for example, that contain instructions and/or ultimatums. Through the constituency office, you work with bureaucracy to deal with the problem.

Sometimes people come into my riding office who didn't vote for me. I tell them that I'm not there just to help the people who voted for me. I'm sorry that their guy didn't win, but I'm your MP and I'm happy to serve just the best way I can, whether they agree with me or disagree with me vehemently. That gives me a broad cross-section of opinion.

In my opinion, once you're elected you don't just disappear to Ottawa and assume all of a sudden that you know best. That is a form of arrogance that I've watched for too many years in Ottawa. It does seem to me, however, that once a member of Parliament becomes a member of the government or a Cabinet minister, all of a sudden they're not so sure they want to hear from the people. I love hearing from the people and I will never quit that.

Reg Alcock, **Liberal MP, 1993–Present**

I represent 60,000 voters and 100,000 people. There's a huge diversity of opinions. I send about 60,000 to 80,000 pieces of direct mail out every month to people in my riding. I have a circulation that goes to my advisory network where they get stuff on events that are taking place in the government on a regular basis. Everybody in my riding gets something from me once a month.

There's a sense that there's a great deal of apathy in politics, but I don't believe that's true. I think what there has been is a lot of bad strategy about how you talk to people. I've worked hard since I got elected, giving people ways to become part of the process. I get the largest amount (anywhere from 400 to 800 letters every week) of handwritten mail of any MP in Ottawa, not because I'm terribly magical but because I work at it. I'm very proud of the fact that so many people get involved, but what's more important is that rather than judging my success back home, it drives my agenda in Ottawa. Quite often I'll walk into caucus with a handful of these letters, approach the prime minister and read from them. People read the papers, they follow the news and they know what the issues are, so if we're debating a particular issue in Ottawa, you can be certain I'm going to receive a flood of mail on it from people in my riding. It helps me understand how their opinion fits with the direction it's going.

Suzanne Tremblay, **Bloc Québécois MP, 1993–Present**

I have in my own riding people who earn their living from lumber and they wrote to me and said to be careful with bill C-55 that Sheila Copps (minister of heritage) put in front of the House dealing with magazines and Canadian ownership of them. They said they did not want to have any trouble with the United States and the exportation of lumber, so I was in a position where I had to decide between what was good for them and what was good for Canadians. We discussed C-55 a lot because it presented a problem for many of my colleagues in the caucus who have paper companies in their constituencies. We often have problems in deciding which way to go. Of course we bring a lot of the problems of our constituency to the table, but we also have to think of the whole situation. In that situation I had to choose between the need to protect the culture of Canada and the need to have two or three businessmen continue to have their business go well. Sometimes it's difficult to decide which way is better, but we thought we had to face the cultural challenge of the United States, or it was going to be the end of culture in Canada. We thought it was more important to defend the culture and to be against the United States on the matter of magazines, so we voted with the government on that one.

We have places in our caucus where we discuss what's going to be important for us and what's going to be important for the interests of Quebecers. Most of the time the interests of Quebecers are also the interests of Canadians, so if we get close to the interests of our people, most of the time it has an application elsewhere.

Alan Tonks, Liberal MP, 2000–Present

I think my constituents see my role very clearly as representing their views. But I don't think that they elected me to go into the Cabinet. I do think they expect me to be able to plug into where the power is to implement programs that are in their interest. And that's my role. Getting into Cabinet is not your sole motivation to run for Parliament. Your motivation is to support the program that best serves the needs of your community.

Your ability to translate that need into strong policies within the government caucus is a fundamental part of your job as an MP. There is the specific job to function as a critic for the media and to be a good constituency person, but a huge part of the job is to develop policies in health care, social services and environmental initiatives that are going to make your community strong, and that's the role that a member has to play.

Richard Marceau, Bloc Québécois MP, 1997–Present

In English Canada, the question that I often hear is, "What are you going to do in Ottawa, destroy the country?" They have a lot of trouble understanding why someone who is a sovereigntist would go to Ottawa with a party. The answer you generally must give to the question is that in a democratic system those who are elected must represent the population as much as they can. English

Canadians may not want to hear it, but there are still around 45 percent of people in Quebec who, when you ask them, are in favour of Quebec sovereignty. It is important for these 45 percent to be represented in Ottawa, but before the BQ, sovereigntists had no voice in Ottawa. You could not vote for a Liberal, Conservative, New Democrat or Alliance government because you were not represented. Now sovereigntists, who make up a good part of the population, have a vehicle on the federal scene which represents, which corresponds to, their values, and this vehicle is the Bloc.

There's a sense in parts of Canada that if you're a sovereigntist, you're stupid or mentally deranged. We want people to know that we're not going on a whim or off the deep end. Take Lucien Bouchard, for example. He was portrayed in caricatures as somebody who was mad, very emotional and irrational, whereas the project he represented is very rational with a very solid legal, political and economical basis.

So my job as the "rest of Canada" spokesperson is mainly having a dialogue between me, representing about half of the population of Quebec who are sovereigntists (between 45 and 50 percent, depending on the surveys), and the rest of Canada about the basis of sovereignty. So that the rest of Canada eventually can say, even if they can't agree with it, the idea makes sense.

I can now use my MP's office as a "bully pulpit," to use an expression used by Theodore Roosevelt, to express my views on why Quebec should be an independent country. Having said this, it does not stop me from doing my job as a member at the local level.

At the local level, whenever somebody comes into my office and asks for help, incidentally mentioning that they voted for me, I tell them that it doesn't matter. I feel that once I am elected, I must be at the service of the whole population, so it doesn't matter what political opinions a constituent has. I'm at the service of the people, but I was elected with the understanding that I'm a sovereigntist.

From the interviews I have quoted above, it is evident that everyone has a different understanding of what it means to be an MP today. Has that role changed over time?

As I delved deeper into this issue, I searched out some former and current MPs, as well as some historians of our Parliament, and asked them all what the job of the MP properly is. From what I have learned, it now seems clear that what we are teaching in our schools about the division between Parliament and government is wrong. In fact this distinction is rarely made, which has tragic consequences for Canadian democracy.

The comments in the next few pages made by those who understand Parliament's role and the government's role in this country are key to understanding why Parliament is in such a sorry state today.

Patrick Boyer, Progressive Conservative MP, 1984–1993

I think a lot of Canadians misunderstand the role of a member of Parliament, including many MPs themselves who sense that they are part of government. Parliament is *not* government: Parliament is a separate body. It's our national legislature, and its role is to be involved in law making, dealing with legislation, and holding the government to account on the issues of the day, if it chooses to. And that's not new. William Gladstone said that in England in 1851 when addressing Parliament and some people who thought that they should be having more of a say in running the country. He pointed out that Parliament's role is not to run the country; that is the role of the government. The problem is that people are elected as representatives to Parliament and think that somehow they're part of the government. They are not.

John Williams, Reform and Canadian Alliance MP, 1993–Present

Parliamentarians think they are either part of government or on their way to becoming government. They have forgotten that they are the *accountability instruments* for government.

Unfortunately Canadians haven't been taught that at school. They think that parliamentarians *are* the government. No, we MPs are not the government. The prime minister and the Cabinet and the departments that they manage are the government, while all the other parliamentarians are part of the accountability processes that scrutinize the government. We as MPs have forgotten that. We see ourselves either as part of government or as an opposition to government.

The problem is, there are not enough Canadians focused on the question, "What is my government doing?" Parliament has lost all its authority to hold the government to account. It's lost its control because Parliament is not that accountability mechanism anymore. This means the government gets away with a lot more than they should.

Government is supposed to come to Parliament and say, "Can I do this? Will you pass this piece of legislation for me? Will you authorize this expenditure of money for me?"

Donald Savoie, Author of Governing from the Centre

The priority of a member of Parliament is to get re-elected. A member of Parliament would do everything that he or she can to ensure he or she appears well in the public eye. Having said that, the role of a member of Parliament is not to say, "I will spend money (in my riding)." The proper role of an MP is to hold the government to account for its policies.

John Williams, Reform and Canadian Alliance MP, 1993–Present

Accountability is what keeps people honest and focused. It keeps their minds on the job. In the private sector it is called competition: if you can't meet or beat the competition, you don't stay in business. But the government doesn't have competition and that's a problem. We MPs have to devise other ways to hold the government accountable. We do it by holding their activities up to the spotlight in a public forum so that all Canadians know what the government is up to. If Canadians approve, that's fine, but when government slips up Canadians need to know about that. That's when accountability kicks in.

I say that accountability drives the other issues. It's a debate. More tax; lower tax. Protect the environment; don't worry about the environment. These debates, in their own way, are about accountability. For example, let's take the environment. We explain and demonstrate how the government has failed on the environment at the tar ponds in Sydney, Nova Scotia. It's an absolute disaster of a place, yet people are living there. The government said, "No, we're not even going to bother paying you to move out of there even though it's ridden with cancer-causing agents." The more we put the pressure on the government and say, "This cannot be. We can't expect Canadians to live in that environment and you had better clean the darn place up, too," then it focuses the government and forces them to do something.

Anne Cools, Liberal Senator, 1984–Present

Parliament is really supposed to be the mightiest representative institution of the nation, the high court of the land. It's where the opinions and the views of the nation are brought forward, discussed, debated and voted upon. The conclusions of Parliament are supposed to be the representative opinions of the citizens.

I have to admit that the system is failing in many cases. Parliament, in many instances, is no longer holding ministers responsible or accountable. I wish Parliament would assert itself a lot more in this respect. I'm not telling any tales out of school to say that Parliament is probably in its weakest stage of its entire history. And remember, Parliament is a very ancient institution. I do not believe, in any of my readings of history, that I have ever known Parliament to be so weak.

To state that Parliament is in the weakest state in its history is a serious charge, and not one all current MPs would accept. Anne Cools is a historian of Parliament and a true champion of what the institution could be: her views should not be ignored.

It is fair to say that sometimes it must be difficult for MPs to exercise hindsight and take a reflective look at their job when they are so inextricably linked to the current way the parliamentary system operates. Most current MPs in Parliament clearly believe their role to be useful.

Why has the traditional meaning of the MP's role been lost? Numerous systemic hurdles stand in the way of Parliament's role of holding the government to account.

Government has grown immensely over the past 40 years, both in the number of programs and in the number of employees. Including interest on its debt, in 1960–61 the federal government spent only $6.3 billion to run the entire government; by 2001 the number was $178.5 billion. Taking into account the rate of inflation over those years, if the federal government were the same relative size today as it was in

1961, its budget would be about \$39.3 billion. The growth has been staggering. Is it any wonder our MPs haven't kept up with what the government does? It surely would have been more manageable for MPs to scrutinize, say, 10 government departments back in 1955, than it is to oversee literally hundreds today. Our government is enormous and reaches into almost every realm of our lives. For today's MP, understanding everything about how the government works is an impossibility.

But a chicken-and-egg dilemma seems to be at work here. Has the weakening of Parliament unleashed uncontrollable strength in government? Or has the incredible growth of government over the past three decades led to a weakened Parliament that is unable to deal with the scope and size of the government it is supposed to oversee?

Anne Cools, Liberal Senator, 1984–Present

Parliament has many roles. One of them is obviously the legislative role. Everybody knows that. We pass bills. But what is not so well known is the administrative role, which is the overseeing of every single department of government. So whether it is Justice or Defence or Energy or Health, Parliament has a duty to oversee the administration and the internal, day-to-day running of those departments.

It is fair to say that in our modern, contemporary society, the size of government has grown at an enormous rate. Executives of government have grown and expanded their influence. Yet Parliament has not grown and developed at the same rate.

The business of Parliament is supposedly to contain and control the administration and the government of the nation. That is what it's supposed to do. Yet Parliament has become little more than a legislative machine which pumps out so much legislation. Votes are held every several weeks on an appointed day, when members come running in to vote as they're supposed to.

The concentration of power is slipping away from Parliament to the government. Some of the symptoms may be the same as some of the consequences. But symptoms are perfectly evident. For example, we have legislative bills that are passing daily, in spite of marked opposition from great numbers of the public, or in some cases a majority of the public.

For example, I was part of the famous Senate filibuster on the GST. The Senate at the time adopted a position that the GST was a bad tax. Under the leadership of Senator Allan MacEachern, a former minister of finance, we endeavoured to fight the Mulroney government on that issue. It was pretty evident that the entire country did not want the bill. The public did not want the tax. The Senate said very clearly that it did not want it. At the time Mr. Mulroney opted not to face the public and go to an election. That's what he should have done if he had come into conflict with the upper chamber, the Senate. But he used an unusual section of the BNA Act to appoint an additional set of eight senators and ensure his legislation got passed.

So the consequence of this new concentration of power away from Parliament is that a lot of bad legislation has been passed. People are not getting the kind of quality of governance that they deserve. Parliament needs to take back its powers and to exercise them more vigorously. They need to defend the public's interest.

Donald Savoie, Author of *Governing from the Centre*

The lowly MP struggles a great deal and has a great deal of work to hold the government accountable. They have to put in an incredible amount of effort without the kind of resources that the prime minister or Cabinet has. Also, they are usually concerned with the interests of their constituency because the people back home decide if they're going to be re-elected or not. Hence their attention is divided a great deal. They simply do not have the resources to hold the government accountable on a program because they do not have the time or the expertise to really understand how the program works.

The government has 100,000 public servants or more. They have Crown corporations. They have access to all kinds of consultants, whereas Parliament has only 80 non-partisan policy researchers. You can't really do battle with 80 non-partisan policy researchers serving both the Senate and the House of Commons, trying to hold 100,000-plus public servants and Cabinet to account. So there's a complete mismatch.

Perhaps a parliamentary system is not designed to and cannot work properly when it must oversee a large government. This idea merits Canadians' consideration but is beyond the scope of this book.

Although many citizens may have a bitter taste in their mouths when it comes to politicians, we cannot forget that most of the people who go into the political game are genuinely civic minded. They want to change the system, they want to have influence. They want to help people. In their small ways, they often can.

Many of the MPs we spoke to seemed to be of two minds; they had dual personalities. On the one hand, they criticized the system of government they operated in, claiming Canada's democracy was in jeopardy. On the other, they personally felt they were doing their jobs well.

Alexa McDonough, **Leader of the New Democratic Party**
> There are lots of jokes these days about how members of Parliament and politicians in general are trusted even less than whoever is thought to be at the bottom of the totem pole. I think it's a bum rap but I also understand it. Some of it starts with politicians who get elected to government saying they will do something, and then doing the opposite and appearing to be virtually unaccountable. I think many people are really fed up with governments that are unaccountable and with politicians who act cynically. The result from that, not surprisingly, is a lot of cynicism from the public. But I think that, generally speaking, you will find that most members of Parliament and most provincial members as well — I can say this from my experience provincially — go into public office because they think they can make a difference. And most of them work pretty hard.

Marlene Catterall, **Liberal MP, 1997–Present; Current Government Whip**
> I think that there's no reason any member of Parliament can't feel they've got a full opportunity to influence what the government is doing. That goes for opposition or government, although I suspect you have a little edge if you're a government member. You're not always going to get your way. If I see a bill in front of me with 200 clauses, I can find three or four that I don't like. But if I essentially like what that bill is doing, then I'm going to support it. If it's an improvement, even if it's not perfect, then

I'm going to support it. I don't always get my way — nobody does. But being a member of Parliament gives you an opportunity to be involved with, to be influencing, virtually any subject that you care about. There are lots of vacuums around here, lots of issues that need work done on them. If you bring some talent to this place, find one of those issues and work on it, then you can accomplish what you want to accomplish.

Although these last two interviewees have an optimistic view of how politicians can effect change, brewing frustration over how our political system works is far more prevalent — except among those in power, of course. Perhaps not so surprisingly, Cabinet members and senior members of the ruling party were much more generous than backbenchers with their accolades for how well the Canadian system works.

John Crosbie, Progressive Conservative Cabinet Minister, 1984–1993

Our Parliament is very frustrating for the members because they are, by and large, ineffectual. But as an MP, I wouldn't go home to my district and say, "Look, I'm ineffectual, but I'm the best ineffectual candidate you could send up, so vote for me."

Ordinary members of Parliament — that is, government members who are not in the Cabinet and opposition members — are pretty well powerless and have very little influence. They can still do a job for their constituents — straightening out this man's unemployment insurance problem or this woman's rent problem — but they don't have much influence in the party or on policy, and they're a very frustrated group.

Bill Blaikie, New Democratic MP, 1979–Present

There is a long-running frustration for members of Parliament that goes back to the 1980s and before. It's that members of Parliament don't have the power that the people who elect them think they have, or think they should have. But that is what people understand as a democracy — that at some point members of Parliament can actually hold the government to account.

MPs search for meaning in their lives and if the meaning is removed in terms of holding the government accountable, it has to pop up somewhere else. I think MPs deal more on the advocacy issues now and less on the accountability and spending issues in Parliament. There is now more playing the role as ombudsman for their voters, in other words, going to bat for various disadvantaged groups or individuals.

So this sense of powerlessness that members of Parliament have is related not just to the fact that they themselves have so little power, but also to the fact that Parliament itself has too little power. This is the larger democratic issue that parliamentary reform needs to tackle if it is really going to get to the root of the frustration that members and the public feel about politics.

Peter Dobell, Director, The Parliamentary Centre[1]

That members of Parliament now have less influence in how decisions are taken should be of concern to voters, but I think a number of people say, "That's beyond me." The people who have more concerns are the members of Parliament themselves. I mean, it's embarrassing for many of them. They fight a campaign. They say, particularly the new ones, that they're going to Ottawa to change the system. That's what happened when the Reform Party came in 1993. But they discovered that not only could they not change it, they've begun to conform to it. Because that's the way the place works.

Reg Alcock, Liberal MP, 1993–Present

As an MP in the House of Commons, I am the tool right now, for better or worse, through which citizens exercise their voice in the affairs of the country. The central job I have is to ensure that the structures that provide voice and rights to people are strong and healthy.

What the House of Commons doesn't do is work in a way that's consistent with the real world. As a result, it is afraid to exercise authority. That's a huge problem that we've got to solve. It makes the MP's job in the House tough. The House of Commons is not an easy place. It's tough to drive things through and to build a consensus. I think that situation will always be there.

There is a loss of authority in the House of Commons. This has meant that some of the big instruments of a government,

the executive (the prime minister and Cabinet) and the departments no longer use the instruments of the citizens — the MPs
— because they no longer see relevance in the House.

George Baker, Liberal MP, 1974–2002

The power of a single member of Parliament in Canada has
eroded considerably over the years. There was a time when any
MP could actually make the government accountable. Today,
under our rules, an MP can't hold up Parliament, can't stop the
proceedings. The party in charge can stifle and control the
input and power of an individual member of Parliament. That
doesn't mean that the Canadian House of Commons is less efficient. In some ways it's more efficient. But where does that leave
the individual MP?

Dennis Mills, Liberal MP, 1988–Present

Traditionally, the executive of any government is the central
power. It has a huge amount of influence on the agenda, style
and momentum of the government. I am not debating that.
What we are talking about here is a sense of balance. In the
House of Commons we are all elected to reflect the needs and
wishes of our constituents. If an executive becomes insensitive
to those needs, then it doesn't create a positive dynamic. The
pendulum has swung to a point where MPs are essentially nothing more than voting machines. It is frustrating because that
attitude is not what the life of an MP is all about.

The issue of making the role of a member of Parliament
more meaningful is so that members could provide better service to their constituents and the public. There was a meeting in
the Railway Committee Room led by Peter Dobell, the director
of the Parliamentary Centre, who was talking about parliamentary reform. Clifford Lincoln, a Liberal MP from
Montreal, stood up and said, "The whole place needs to be
blown to smithereens, and we have to start all over." I got up
and made some interventions. I said that, essentially, lobbyists
are listened to on Parliament Hill more than members of
Parliament are.

Peter MacKay, **Progressive Conservative MP, 1997–Present**

In the grand scheme of things it's discouraging for the members who are here. I believe that we will not get the quality in individuals coming forward to serve in the House of Commons if they feel that their voice is not going to be heard, or they're not going to be able to make a substantial change on behalf of their constituents. To that end it's very unfortunate.

Patrick Boyer, **Progressive Conservative MP, 1984–1993**

What we're seeing with the evolution of Canada's Parliament is very well demonstrated by the 180-degree reversal in what's required when Canadian men and women wearing the Canadian maple leaf on their soldier's uniforms are sent beyond our shores bearing arms. Let me give you the long view of Canadian history.

There was always a policy from the very beginning, from colonial times, that no soldiers would be sent outside Canadian borders without authorization by Parliament, the legislative assembly. The first time that this happened after Confederation was the time of the Boer War in South Africa. Wilfrid Laurier, who was leading the official Opposition, urged that there be a referendum in Canada to authorize the sending of our soldiers to South Africa. This was not to be merely a vote by Parliament, which Laurier and all the other leaders of the day knew was a necessary precursor for any of our military personnel to leave the country, but a step beyond typical politics, by taking the issue to all the Canadian people. The view then, as it ought to be today, was that in a democracy no question requiring a decision can be too big for direct participation by the people.

We saw that same approach continue in August of 1914, when Prime Minister Borden was with his wife on a vacation in Muskoka, after years of unrelenting work in Ottawa. What he thought might have been a week of great Muskoka vacation time was cut short because the storm clouds of war had broken over Europe. He immediately went back to Ottawa by train, Parliament was summoned and a vote was taken on a resolution to declare war and to commit the military of Canada to service overseas.

The same approach continued into World War II. The Mackenzie King Liberal government, having won re-election in 1940 on a pledge that there would not be conscription for overseas military service, discovered by 1942 that the direction of the war seemed to require conscription. So honour-bound was Prime Minister Mackenzie King to his mandate from the people that, again, in the middle of the war, his government went back to the country with a national referendum. It was a ballot question directly asking the Canadian people whether they would release the government from its prior commitment against conscription. Yes or no? That's how serious it was.

The Korea campaign represented a turning point in which we begin to see a shift toward more "executive management" of these decisions, in which the Canadian Parliament was not as centrally involved.

By the time of the Gulf War in 1990, there I was, parliamentary secretary at National Defence, attending a conference up at Lake Couchiching. I was standing beside a ranking officer in the Canadian Armed Forces and we were both watching Prime Minister Mulroney on television. He was not meeting Parliament in session to vote on whether our Armed Forces were going to be dispatched overseas, but at a press conference announcing to all of us and to the world that a commitment had been made to dispatch ships and planes into the Gulf War.

Part of the reason that Canadians today feel so distanced from their government is that we've had a run for 30 or 40 years of leaders who thought that the way of the government was to make the big announcement. Don't do it in Parliament, do it at a press conference. Here's the big announcement, folks, and "Oh, guess what? The prime minister just announced something."

I think these examples document how Parliament has totally been eclipsed and has been made irrelevant to any of these decisions. It leaves wide open the question: if Parliament isn't part of the process, where in the name of democracy in Canada is accountability for the government being enforced?

Peter Dobell, **Director, The Parliamentary Centre**

Cabinet ministers no longer listen to what MPs say in the House of Commons. They may pay some attention to what they say in their party's caucus, or they may accept that a member comes in and has a private meeting or talks to them on the floor of the House.

When members of Parliament participate in discussion of a policy issue, they should be allowed to approach it as intelligent individuals drawing on their experience. When they come to a common decision on a national issue, they should be listened to. That doesn't happen now. From the point of view of the member, that is what is so frustrating. It's particularly frustrating for opposition members because the ruling government members do have the opportunity, through their party caucuses, of having occasionally some influence on what the government is going to do.

On the other hand, the government members have the disadvantage that they are discouraged from speaking their own mind. When they are asked to speak in the House, they are often given the text by an aide to the minister on the issue on which they're speaking, and they're told, "That's what you've got to say." If they have a matter that really troubles them, it's hard for them to get to the floor. The opposition members have the satisfaction of getting up and attacking, but they have no influence. Both of them, for different reasons, have frustrations.

Is this true? Are MPs really told by their political parties what to say in the House of Commons? Are MPs' speeches written by others? Two veteran members of Parliament, Patrick Boyer and Ted McWhinney, who come from different sides of the political fence, confirmed the truth of these statements. It seems that the House of Commons has sunk to being a place where speeches are read to defend a government line or to oppose it.

Patrick Boyer, **Progressive Conservative MP, 1984–1993**

For many years, when I was in Parliament, people would be handed speeches written by the senior policy speechwriters of government departments. If it was a transport bill, a defence bill, if it was something to do with agriculture, these potted speeches were handed out, and the term used was "modules." There would be various paragraphs or modules that you could move around, but there were key messages. And of course, who crafted these? There were speechwriters, working in concert with opinion polls, who had pretty much determined where the tolerances were for the Canadian public to be receptive to this message.

Ted McWhinney, Liberal MP, 1993–2000

When I was in the Fisheries Ministry I was parliamentary secretary before I went to Foreign Affairs. The ministry used to write these speeches and they'd start out with platitudes — "Canada stands on so many oceans, and the frontier extends from one ocean to another ..." — and I said, "This is junk, why do you do this? Who does it?" The answer was, "Retired civil servants are paid to do them." I said, "Why do they write this junk?" The answer was, "They seem to think MPs expect this."

Patrick Boyer, Progressive Conservative MP, 1984–1993

Often parliamentarians are simply filling up the debate space, talking out measures that may have been introduced by opposition and that would challenge the government's position. It's kind of a Canadian version of a parliamentary filibuster to have these innocuous speeches just filling up space.

In terms of how these speeches are written and also how they're delivered in Parliament, it's kind of fun. I suppose it's why the Shakespearean festival at Stratford is such a booming success. People like theatre in this country — we've seen our national Parliament become a version of political theatre. And the actors and actresses are doing tolerably well in front of the cameras with the scripts that have been handed to them.

As I remember, one would finish reading the speech only to be succeeded by another parliamentarian reading kind of a continuation of the same text — inasmuch as it had been crafted out of the same minister's office by the same speechwriter, complimenting one another on their fine thoughts and their great contributions.

Now, if I'm an MP and, either in the House of Commons or somewhere at a public event across the country, I'm taking and reading one of these speeches, what's wrong with this picture? Well, what's wrong is that it's not me. The person that's written these words that I'm mouthing has not been at the caucus meetings and heard the cut and thrust of philosophical debate on these issues. He or she has not been around the electoral district. No, this is someone who is a wordsmith, good at crafting the nice phrase. It's someone who knows what the opinion polls state on the issue of the day. It's someone who knows the position the government has already arrived at and is trying to sell it to the public.

So the result is that we have seen the public representatives in our national Parliament rendered into vacuous ciphers. There may be different marionettes whose strings are being pulled, but the same play is being performed. And that is not a Parliament. That is not representation of the people. That is a complete functional abdication of the role of being a representative of the people of this country in our national public life.

Ted McWhinney, Liberal MP, 1993–2000

Personally I had a rule when I spoke in the House of Commons: I only spoke on the issues where I had something to say. Yet the research bureau attached to the political parties, and operating through the government whip's office, prepared many of the speeches on both sides of the House of Commons. I made a point of reading the speeches just to make sure I knew what government policy was so I didn't get out of the party line unconsciously. I liked to know what they said, but I wouldn't use them. I gave my own speeches, and the whip accepted that.

Parliament used to be a place of true debate. Now MPs read speeches and compliment the ministers while rubber-stamping issues presented by the government. How can MPs properly oversee the government in this atmosphere? One cannot help but become cynical about how politics works in Canada.

Sadly, when I traced back the changes to the traditional role of the MP, I found out that the House of Commons wasn't always like this.

During the decades leading up to the early 1960s, MPs did play an important role. The erosion of this role has occurred gradually over the last 40 or so years.

Peter Dobell, Director, The Parliamentary Centre

To appreciate all the changes to the role of a member of Parliament, you have to look back to the 1950s. Back then members of Parliament were the primary source of information on how the people in the region in which they lived thought about public issues. They were the avenue Cabinet ministers used to find out how people think about issues. For that reason, back then Cabinet ministers would normally attend most debates in the House of Commons. This meant that when a member of Parliament was speaking, he or she felt that what they were saying would be listened to and possibly have an influence.

Patrick Boyer, Progressive Conservative MP, 1984–1993

If you go back and read *Hansard* up to the 1950s or early 1960s, what you'll find is a record of very informed and intelligent discussion by parliamentarians about issues. Cabinet ministers would bring new legislation before Parliament and explain what problems were necessitating it. They explained why they were trying to address issues with specific measures and why they thought the measures were going to be successful. You would also read the record of opposition members and members on the government side sharing their points of view and considerations on such matters from their own experience. *Hansard* up to that point documents the House of Commons as being a place where thoughtful adults were speaking together with the objective of being law makers and generating legislation that was going to be the most effective at that point in time for Canada. It truly was a Parliament: a gathering of mature, informed, seasoned Canadians with different outlooks, discussing, debating and crystallizing points of view on the issues that would affect the future of this country.

Today, do we have that? Not at all. What I found during my time in Parliament were speeches crafted on opinion polls, based on policy that had already been decided by the government and that was being laid out as the perfect solution to the problem at hand. No doubt. No hesitation. It's forced through: "You accept it, and by the way, backbenchers, fall in line and support it. And incidentally, if you're on the other side of the House of Commons, fall in line and oppose it." This is a fairly dumb exercise for mature adults in a self-governing democracy.

George Baker, Liberal MP, 1974–2002

In my 28 years in the House of Commons, I've watched power being drained from the member of Parliament. Years ago it was very common to see an MP actually hold up proceedings, using various means. Thirty years ago, as an MP you could stand up and the Speaker of the House would recognize you. All of the MPs would be popping up like jackrabbits, and the Speaker would select someone to ask a question. Today you go into the House and the Speaker calls a name. The MP says, "Oh, is that my name?" because it's on the list.

An MP's power has eroded in stages. Rule changes have eroded the MP's power to the point that if you're not on the whip's list, or you're out of favour with your political party, you can't even speak, let alone ask a question in Question Period. Under present procedures in the House of Commons, all that an MP can do is refuse unanimous consent on every occasion that he or she wishes. That's just about the only thing left.

Patrick Boyer, Progressive Conservative MP, 1984–1993

It didn't happen overnight that somebody got out of bed and said, "I think I'll convert from being a robust, thinking-for-myself Canadian and just become a lackey on a leash for the system." It doesn't happen that way. But a couple of the long-term trends were a quest for efficiency in government, which we saw through the 1960s and 1970s, and the great force of personal political ambition.

Now, dealing with that first one. If you were running the Government of Canada through the 1960s and 1970s, spending was going up by billions of dollars from year to year, and you're hiring, not thousands more, but tens of thousands more people into the public service. And you've got programs for everything that moves in the country. There's a point where you start to say, "We've got to get efficient about this huge organization." And rightly so. But a part of our national government is Parliament. So what happened was, especially when Michael Pitfield was secretary of the Cabinet under Prime Minister Trudeau, there were a lot of new proposals brought in to streamline and make government more effective, including, for example, the way that Parliament always seemed to talk about things endlessly. So rules were brought in to limit the amount of speech time that MPs would have.

Combined with that is the reality that a lot of people go into political life because they are ambitious to advance their careers. The great thing about the Parliament in England is that there's about 700 parliamentarians. So most of those folks know they're never going to get to be in the Cabinet, and never even going to get to be chairs of parliamentary committees. They're cool about that, and they just spend time being parliamentarians — questioning things, running around holding officials to account and what have you.

Our Parliament has 300 members. A number are in opposition, so you might have 160 to 200 of them on the government's side. By the time you've got 30 or 40 in Cabinet, and then another 30 or 40 as parliamentary secretaries, and then another dozen or two chairing committees, and then some others being deputy chairs of committees, plus the whips and so on, there's only a relatively small number of parliamentarians left on the government's side who aren't in positions of power.

And you've got to remember that every chair of a committee sees herself or himself as next becoming a junior Cabinet minister. Every junior Cabinet minister sees himself becoming a more senior Cabinet minister. And most senior Cabinet ministers aspire to become prime minister. So what we have going on in our Parliament is this wonderful game of political ambition that's motivating people every step of the way. They're learning how to hold their tongue, how to be polite and deferential to the one who can appoint them higher up. So they're not becoming critics. I've seen this so many times. Even though they've got fundamentally different views on what's going down, they don't express them because they don't want to imperil their advancement to a higher position.

So those two factors taken together have resulted in our Parliament being really just a little drama centre, where nothing of true significance is actually going on.

Unbounded political ambition and the size of government: these are the two stakes in the heart of Parliament and our MPs' role in it.

What is interesting about Patrick Boyer's final comment is his emphasis on just how important the party system has become over the years to the ambitions of MPs. Being loyal to the party in power, or to the opposition party fighting to get into power, has become the supreme raison d'être for MPs. It keeps people in line by focusing their attention on means at the expense of ends.

The rise of "team politics" has ensured that individual MPs and freethinkers are kept on the outside of political parties, or that they are chastised for sabotaging the party line everyone in a party must follow. Sadly, our Parliament doesn't seem designed to take the pounding party politics has inflicted upon it. The lowly voters must hope that the MP they vote for is in good standing with his or her party; if not, he or she will inevitably be sidelined.

NOTES

1. The Parliamentary Centre is a non-profit corporation that works to strengthen legislatures as vital institutions for good governance.

CHAPTER 2

The Rise of Party Politics:
Our Collective Partisan Blindness

If you want to be an MP in Canada today, being part of a political party is mandatory. Quite simply, if you are not aligned with a political party you won't get elected. Some MPs have maintained that they were elected solely due to their personal popularity with their constituents, but other than John Nunziata, very few MPs in the history of Parliament have been elected without a party affiliation. As Liberal House Leader Don Boudria explained in his on-camera interview with us, "If the Canadian people wanted 301 independent MPs, why did they elect zero? In the 2000 election, 1,500 independent candidates ran and none of them won." He's right: as voters we are continually searching for a party to put our X beside.

Given that there is systemic adherence to political parties, how does the party system affect MPs as parliamentarians? There is an important distinction here. Everyone acknowledges that an MP must respect a commitment to the party platform that he or she was elected on. But what about an MP's role in overseeing the same government that he or she belongs to? We must remember that parliamentarians are also elected to play an indispensable role in our system (even if they are on the ruling party side): *to scrutinize the government*. MPs must also appease different regional, cultural, social and economic perspectives to achieve a national consensus, which in some cases might not sit well with their party.

Has the enforcement of party discipline and the influence of political parties helped or hindered Canada's Parliament? Ask yourself: if you were an MP, would the current parliamentary system demean your integrity? Is the party line necessary?

John Williams, Reform and Canadian Alliance MP, 1993–Present

In the concept of Parliament the parties do not exist. Parliamentarians are MPs who support the government and those who oppose the government. But the concept of Parliament is not broken down into clear party divisions, that "these MPs" support the government and "these MPs" are in the opposition. It talks about parliamentarians supporting the government's initiatives, and if the government can carry the day in the House of Commons, then it has the confidence to govern. But this has evolved into this tight party discipline that says if you are a member of the government, you will vote their way regardless of whether you like it or not. That allows them to stay in power, even though perhaps they maybe really do not enjoy the confidence of the government or the confidence of Parliament; by the vote it appears that they do.

Patrick Boyer, Progressive Conservative MP, 1984–1993

We have "partyism" in Parliament. We've carried what we do on the hockey rink into our Parliament. You're either wearing that red sweater or that blue sweater. And if you're wearing that other-coloured sweater, we're going to skate you into the boards and maybe even elbow you in the corner because you're on the wrong team. We've carried that mentality into our parliamentary life, to its great detriment.

Stanley Hartt, Former Chief of Staff to Prime Minister Brian Mulroney

When the voters choose their members and they give overwhelming majorities to one party, the voters have said, "We want you to have all that power." Nobody makes up the rules after he gets into office. The voters know how powerful the executive council or the Cabinet is in our system when they vote. When they give an absolutely overwhelming majority to one party, they know they're electing, in effect, a dictatorship for four years. That's because of party discipline and the fact that we have the rule that you have to maintain the "confidence of the House," that is, if a bill doesn't pass, you have to resign as the ruling government.

Citizens know that the prime minister and his Cabinet will use that power over the members in order to get them to vote for what the Cabinet decides policy ought to be and they'll brook no contradictions.

Don Newman,
Senior Political Analyst, Canadian Broadcasting Corporation

The government considers most votes a question of "confidence." The ultimate confidence test is of course the budget. But the fact is, the budget is *the* confidence motion, and even if we move to more free votes, we will never have a free vote on the budget. The system just doesn't work that way. If the government cannot get the support of the House of Commons on how the money is going to be spent, well, then it has to resign, there has to be an election or the governor general has to invite someone else to form a government. It was the no-confidence motion on the budget that finished the Joe Clark government in 1979.

Stanley Hartt, Former Chief of Staff to Prime Minister Brian Mulroney

The disdain of parliamentarians for the Prime Minister's Office (PMO) comes from the fact that the PMO's job is to make the prime minister look good even when he's doing tough things. They need to convey the impression that the party is still united, that what the party is doing is good. So if a member disagrees with something, sometimes he gets the feeling that this message is conveyed to him on behalf of the prime minister in a way that is inconsistent with his rights as a democratically elected representative.

What the member of Parliament is supposed to do about that is not fight with the PMO. What they're supposed to do is go to caucus and say, "Cabinet has presented us with a legislative initiative that we, many of us, disagree with. And we don't want that bill to go forward as a government bill." It's in caucus that that discussion takes place.

There is a mechanism for MPs to convey disagreements and it's called the caucus. It's behind closed doors.

Marlene Catterall, Liberal MP, 1997–Present; Current Government Whip

The party in power got elected based on the promises of the leader. All the other candidates can't suddenly turn around after the election and say, "Oops, I was wrong. I'm not a Liberal. I don't support those programs." The second point is that when a bill comes to Parliament, it's already been discussed at great length within our caucus. Members who have a problem with it have an opportunity to work at those problems with the ministers. Ministers are responsive, and if they're not, the prime minister makes sure they are so that when legislation comes to the House, it's something that we've all worked on. It's a product of the team, not just of an individual minister.

Reg Alcock, Liberal MP, 1993–Present

Politics is a team sport. Here, if I fully understand 30 percent of the votes I make, I'm doing well. This is a very, very complex business, so we organize ourselves into groups. I have developed expertise in certain areas and I call upon the group to support me and I deliver support. That's what being in a party or a parliamentary system is all about. We sign on to a certain set of principles when we run for a party.

I chose to be a Liberal. I did it because I share a certain value set that gets represented by that party, as did the Reform/Alliance guys and the NDP. So the fact that we vote together shouldn't come as a huge surprise. Now, it's true that there is whipping on three votes a year that are truly confidence votes. There are other votes where the government can say, "Here's the confidence vote. If it fails we will have an election." But there are only three real confidence votes. The rest of the time you vote because you're with the group. You dance with the one who brung you.

Stanley Hartt, **Former Chief of Staff to Prime Minister Brian Mulroney**
You don't disagree with your party in public because the system is based on maintaining the loyalty of a majority of members. So when your loyalty becomes questioned and you reveal that publicly, you're already raising doubts in the mind of the governor general about whether or not the prime minister really does have a majority in the House of Commons.

So it's not unknown for the Prime Minister's Office staff to go and sit with a member and say, "On this bill we'd like to talk to you about the fact that you've been known to have said — first privately and now a little bit publicly — that you disagree, and we'd like to talk you out of that. Not necessarily because you don't have the right to disagree — there's a time and place to disagree — but once caucus has decided to back a bill, you're supposed to stand up and vote with your party, on matters of confidence."

And remember, we still have not in this country redefined what a "confidence matter" is. Almost all government-initiated bills, and certainly all money bills, are deemed to be matters of confidence.

In grade school Canadians are taught that responsible government means the government, as represented by Cabinet and the prime minister, must hold the "confidence" of a majority of all the *other* elected MPs in the House of Commons in order to retain office. This confidence is gauged by votes, and thus the Cabinet ministers (the executive of government) must perpetually secure a majority of the votes of members of Parliament. So, for example, when the government calls for a "confidence motion" it has to ensure that more MPs vote to support the motion than vote against it. If a greater number of MPs vote against the motion, the government is defeated; Parliament must be dissolved and an election called. This is what happened in 1979 to Prime Minister Joe Clark when his minority government lost the parliamentary vote on the proposed budget. Clark was forced to step down and call another election.

This was a rare event in Canadian history. Since 1980 we have had nothing but strong majority governments, where one party has held well in excess of 50 percent of the seats in the House of Commons. Yet during the last 20-odd years we have seen more so-called confidence votes than ever. Indeed, over the past several decades government use of unnecessary confidence votes has been excessive. Now almost every controversial vote has become a question of "confidence" — or so says the ruling party. This threat is a sham of what the convention of confidence is intended to be. To suggest that MPs would bring down the government for voting freely (without party discipline) on say, gay rights, foreign aid, the Young Offender's Act, or any of the other sticky issues we are faced with today is absurd. Just because an MP may vote against his or her party on one of these issues, and in the process justly represent his or her voters back home, does not mean that the MP wants the government to fall and an election to be called.

Free votes and real parliamentary discussion on these sorts of issues are what Parliament is supposed to be all about. These debates and votes are vital to the shaping of a national consensus on the future of this country.

Currently so many votes are considered confidence votes that the government is telling its members to "vote for us or else." This of course puts immense pressure on back-bench MPs to toe the party line. But if all issues in Parliament are simply voted on to rubber-stamp what the government has already decided, then hasn't Parliament simply become an appendage to government rather than the legitimate democratic body that oversees it?

When Parliament is dominated by the party system, power is concentrated in the various party groups. The weekly Wednesday meetings of each political party, which are called caucus meetings, are where all the decisions are made. The House of Commons provides little more than the venue for holding the final vote.

Don Newman,
Senior Political Analyst, Canadian Broadcasting Corporation

Certainly within the political parties the caucus has replaced the House of Commons as a place of open discussion. When legislation comes to the floor of the House of Commons, you only have to listen to the first speaker from each of the five parties and you have a pretty good idea how the parties are going to vote. You don't have to listen to the other speakers.

The caucus is where the backbenchers get a chance to talk to the Cabinet ministers and voice their opinions. At the end of the caucus meeting the prime minister sums up what he has

45

heard, but he doesn't necessarily have to follow their advice. The bottom line is that MPs, while they don't have as much power as they would like, do have power in the caucus, and the public just doesn't get to see them exercise it.

Peter MacKay, **Progressive Conservative MP, 1997–Present**

There has to be a change in attitude for members of Parliament, backbenchers in particular, to feel that they are a more important part of the process and have more power. That change would include more free votes in the House of Commons. There's a lot of talk about these things, but rarely do we see the leadership of a ruling party completely relinquish the reins of the party whip when it comes to voting on matters of conscience. Free votes are far too rare. In my memory there's been very few occasions where there's been a completely free vote.

Another change that needs to happen is, for example, to have all private members' bills votable, give members of Parliament a greater ability to participate in debate and level out the time that members are given to debate certain issues.

Judy Wasylycia-Leis, **New Democratic MP, 1997–Present**

I have watched Liberals begin their terms in Parliament saying they were going to fight to eradicate poverty, fight for the compensation of hepatitis C victims and fight for the homeless. In the end their hands are tied because of government policy and because of a very tight voting structure. I have talked to some Liberal backbenchers who are frustrated because they get instructions on how to act, how to vote, what to say, and really have no freedom to influence the process. Jean Chrétien doesn't allow for much dissent within the ranks.

My biggest concerns are the decisions made in the Prime Minister's Office and decisions made at the level of the non-elected World Trade Organization which are never brought before Parliament. Global corporate forces have such a powerful agenda that this prime minister and this government are prepared to sacrifice democracy and bypass parliamentary representation. I saw a whole number of critical bills come before Parliament and just when the debate was getting interesting, just when people started to provide input and have an impact on the issues, the prime minister brought in closure, which shut down the debate and forced the bill through Parliament.

I have noticed a big change over the last several years in the whole democratic process. I think there has been a deliberate attempt to circumvent the democratic institutions in which MPs and Parliament have been increasingly disregarded.

Don Boudria,
Liberal MP, 1984–Present; Current Government House Leader

We weren't elected as independent MPs. We were elected as partisan MPs. I was elected as a Liberal. Each MP was elected as part of a team. I was elected as part of the Liberal group, with the platform of the *Red Book*. We're expected to come here and espouse the views that we expressed during the election campaign, and not to say, "Look, I'm not bound by any of this stuff. We said it to get elected, but now I can do what I like." That's just not how it works. So people expect their MPs to speak as part of a group, to espouse and defend the views that they stated during the election campaigns and that are presented by the political parties from time to time.

Marlene Catterall, Liberal MP 1997–Present; Current Government Whip

It's like a family discussion: "Where are we going on holidays?" We can all have our opinion, but once a decision is made we all go on the same holiday. This is a team sport, and you're accountable to the public for supporting the team you were elected to. And the government's responsible for fulfilling its promises to Canadians. It's that simple.

Alan Tonks, Liberal MP, 2000–Present

My granddad, who was a Progressive Conservative, once told me that you choose your party and you stay with that party. If it's wrong, you change the party, but you don't change parties. You have to bring in every power that you have to get on with the next issue, within the context of the party, because the party isn't always totally wrong or totally right in any given instance. At the end of the day, because we have a democracy in which the majority must rule in every sense, one must support the elected party's position and not undermine it.

I am a Liberal. My values are Liberal and I've always been Liberal. This constituency has traditionally voted Liberal because they believed in those values, and I represent them. I can be the voice for this constituency, not only to bring it better government and services, but also to do that for cities across the country. Being a part of the government side will bring more influence and more support to my riding (York South–Weston) than if I weren't, and I can play a stronger role, within the Liberal caucus and within the government, than someone who is on the outside looking in.

John Nunziata, Liberal MP, 1984–1996; Independent MP 1996–2000

"Team player" is code for a trained seal. If being a team player means being a trained seal and an irrelevant government backbencher, then who wants to be one? The prime minister exercises power in a dictatorial fashion, punishing MPs that don't toe the party line.

Patrick Boyer, Progressive Conservative MP, 1984–1993

We've seen the ascendance of organized political party discipline, the intense role of the party whips controlling who says what and when and how, on all issues from foreign policy down to something like satellite dishes or acreage payments for wheat farmers.

It doesn't matter what's going through Parliament, there's a strict line that's adhered to. There was a time when people, including in this country, would invoke the name of Edmund Burke and his great speech to the electors of Bristol, in which Burke said that an elected representative owes the people who elect him or her the best of his or her conscience and independent thinking. Point to examples in recent memory of conscience and independent thinking in the Canadian House of Commons. If you can find them, you're also going to find examples of people who were placed under the thumb of the whip, the party structure and the party leadership. So in fact we have less responsible government in practice today than probably going back to the days of the Family Compact, the Château

Clique, Lord Durham's report and the invention of this concept that we should, in fact, have an accountable executive. Today we do not have that.

Peter Dobell, Director, The Parliamentary Centre

With the current system in Ottawa, the political party in power tells back-bench MPs how to vote. In Britain's Parliament they have a number of levels of voting discipline. If it's something on which they campaigned and where they had taken a strong position, then the government members are expected to support that and are in trouble if they don't. That's called a three-line whip. Then you have what they call two-line or one-line, and that means some encouragement to vote with the government party, but not an order. You wouldn't be in real trouble if you didn't do it. Particularly if you could demonstrate why your vote was different. I think our problem in Canada is that we haven't given our MPs enough latitude in voting. The power is coming from on top. Once the decision is taken, MPs are expected to vote the party line.

Suzanne Tremblay, Bloc Québécois MP, 1993–Present

In politics, if you don't go along with the party line, you may be excluded or punished. I don't think doing that is worthwhile because I think I can be more useful acting freely as a spokesperson for Canadians. In that case I think it's better for me to stay in my office rather than to stand up and openly vote against my party. Look what happened with Mr. Nunziata and other members of the Liberal Party who decided to vote against the government. The political parties don't support this kind of rebellion. So we try to stay low profile when we decide against something. I think it's more important for me to be able to wake up the next morning and be happy to live with who I am, rather than my conscience telling me what I should have done.

If there is a party line that I cannot support at all, I won't be in the House to vote against it. I will stay in my office instead. If a journalist asks me if I was not in the House because I was against the vote, I would say yes. I wouldn't have any problem with that, but it's very rare.

Frankly, sometimes I go in to vote on something and I'm given a paper and told that we are going to be for that bill for such-and-such reason, but I never saw the bill before. We all are like this and sometimes when I'm speaking with people from the Liberal Party and they ask me why I voted for or against something, they discover that they were not aware that there were problems in the law. They just approved it because they had to since they're backbenchers and they don't have a clue about what they're doing there, except voting the way the prime minister told them to vote.

Stanley Hartt, Former Chief of Staff to Prime Minister Brian Mulroney

If an MP is out of line with the party, he or she will feel the heavy hand of the Prime Minister's Office, which will say, "Wait a second, buddy, we sign your nomination papers for the next election. Funding from the centre comes through the central party organism with which we liaise. If you're not going to help the party, why should the party help you?" And sometimes that heavy hand makes MPs feel unhappy.

MPs are rewarded for toeing the party line. That's how party committee chairmanships are given out. That's how parliamentary secretary jobs are given out. Ultimately that's how Cabinet jobs are given out. You will find, invariably, no matter what party is in office, that if an MP is being difficult, doesn't agree with his party's policy, is consistently out of line with the whips, the House leader and the PMO — and says so publicly — that MP is not going to get promoted to one of those plum jobs.

Peter Dobell, Director, The Parliamentary Centre

The executive is good at keeping MPs in line in the House. First of all, have you ever seen how they vote? They stand up, one after another. Their names are called and they go down the line. It takes enormous courage for someone to fail to stand up or to stand up and say no if all of his colleagues are saying yes. That's one form of discipline.

George Baker, Liberal MP, 1974–2002

The MPs know that their entire effectiveness as members of Parliament is held in the hands of the party leader and the whip.

Their power can be thwarted if they're out of sync with their leader or their party. It means an MP has to be in good standing with the party, the leader and the whip to get on Question Period and to speak in the House of Commons. Where did we get the custom that every question asked in the House of Commons is decided upon by the whip of each political party?

There are whole lists of sanctions that can be brought to bear against a maverick MP in our political party system. For example, MPs must be in good standing to get on the committees that they want to join. The opposition parties and the government can choose on which committees backbenchers or private members can sit. There's an election for the chair of the committee, but these matters are really decided beforehand by the executive. If you aren't in favour of the government of the day, then you aren't going to be the chair of the committee. Also, a member must be in good standing to go on trips that examine policies overseas.

Peter Dobell, **Director, The Parliamentary Centre**
What other things can they do? Well, they can remove someone from his committee. There was a rather dramatic example some years ago, when Warren Allmand, an MP with about 25 years' seniority, was chairman of a major committee. He was simply withdrawn from the committee. So that's another discipline. A third form of discipline? They could not expect to be included in a delegation travelling abroad. Fourth, an MP might be looking for some assistance in their constituency. It would become harder if they were on the government's side.

John Nunziata, **Liberal MP, 1984–1996; Independent MP 1996–2000**
We all know what happens. If you're not a good boy or a good little girl, then instead of going on one of the more sexy committees, like the justice committee or the finance committee or foreign affairs, you're put on the library committee. If you're not a good little boy or girl, you're not going to go on any foreign trips and you're not going to get invited to 24 Sussex for a state visit. In other words, MPs are punished if they don't toe the party line. I know that. I've been there, done that and got the T-shirt.

John Nunziata is the most vocal and well-known MP in the history of Parliament to vote against the budget of his own party. The issue was the goods and services tax. To this day Nunziata maintains that he did not vote against the government in 1996 with the intention of defeating it. He maintains he was simply trying to vote with his conscience and keep the promise he believed his party made to voters in the previous election: that the Liberals, if elected, would scrap the GST. Prime Minister Chrétien had a different opinion. He moved quickly, sending a message to other Liberal MPs by promptly removing Nunziata from the party he had supported for decades.

John Nunziata, **Liberal MP, 1984–1996; Independent MP 1996–2000**

It was kind of strange to get booted. I was one of only 40 Liberal MPs in 1984 that were elected. Together with Brian Tobin, Sheila Copps and Jean Chrétien, we helped rebuild the party. I remember Brian Mulroney saying the Liberal Party was dead. I received a fax a few days after I voted against the budget from Jean Chrétien, saying that I was no longer a part of the caucus.

It hurt, but in politics the highs are incredibly high and the lows are incredibly low and justice ultimately is done. One of the lows was the day I received the fax kicking me out of the caucus, but the high was on June 2, 1997, when I beat the Liberal Party. I beat Jean Chrétien when the people of this riding said, "John, what you did was right. You're our representative, we want you to represent us in Canada." I was the only independent elected in Canada and that was one of the incredible highs in my career.

I feel that I've been part of a very unique democratic exercise here in the riding of York South–Weston.

It may have been a unique democratic exercise, but it was also a short-lived hurrah for Nunziata. Despite his huge popularity in Toronto, he was defeated by the Liberal candidate in 2000. The party system that helped Nunziata get elected in 1984 triumphed once again, this time taking out the now independent MP who was such a thorn in its side.

Some may argue that the issue of political party power in our parliamentary system is of small concern because the parties do generally represent Canadians. But is this true? We must remember that less than two percent of the Canadian population actually belongs to a political party. In reality only a very small number of people command the tight institutional control of political parties and the messages they try to sell to the public at voting time.

Take this fact to the government level. We can see that for all intents and purposes the political party system now also controls Parliament. By often heavy-handedly controlling the votes, debates and even the speeches of its party's MPs, the leadership can ensure that MPs follow the strict dictates of the party hierarchy. Sure, the opposition can try to stall legislation, and occasionally government members can debate behind closed doors in caucus (although their success in this realm is open to question), but MPs on the government side will inevitably vote the way their political party asks them to, or suffer the consequences. With such rigid party discipline and with such top-down adherence to one's own party, what has happened to Parliament's role as scrutinizer of the government?

And who has benefited politically from the current situation? The prime minister of course!

CHAPTER 3

From MP to PM:
The Move to Centralized Power

It is often said that political power and the need to control it define the basic bargain between those who govern and those who are governed. As voters and citizens, we convey vast powers to the political executive of the Canadian government: the Cabinet and the prime minister. We grant them our consent to tax, to spend and to create our laws. In return we citizens demand accountability. We expect the government to explain and justify publicly the way it uses its power and to take corrective action when things go wrong. This is the pact between us, the people, and them, the government. In theory this sort of democracy means "government for the people, by the people," but this lofty theory no longer applies in Canada.

Democracy is not supposed to empower political and government leaders to use power for their own benefit. As we have seen in the past two chapters, the MP's role has moved from being an individual tasked with overseeing our government and holding it to account for its action, to being a member of a "team" who is commanded to support that team at all costs.

Just how centralized has power become in Canada? How is that power exercised? What are the consequences? Parliament and MPs have been sidelined by the rise in power of the Cabinet and the prime minister. The form of democracy we have now in Canada is closer to "government by the government, for the government." Parliament and our elected MPs are unable to resist the government's chokehold on power.

What has happened to leadership in the truest sense of the word? Where is the sort of leadership in this country that allows citizens, and MPs as their proxies, to judge our leaders' character and vision for the country on an ongoing basis? Where are the leaders who force Canadians to debate their policies and present a future direction for Canada in our Parliament, without railroading things through? Can we have that sort of leadership with a Parliament where ministers are seldom answerable to the House of Commons and never answerable to a fully functioning Senate?

Joe Clark, Progressive Conservative Leader and Former Prime Minister

The prime minister is virtually all-powerful in our system. If a prime minister leads a majority government, he controls his own political party, so there's not very much internal pressure. He names and fires Cabinet ministers and senior public servants. In some Cabinets I've sat in, there are strong ministers who will stand up to a prime minister. I don't think you get as much of that in the Cabinet of Mr. Chrétien and I think that this tendency has gradually declined with the passage of time. What has happened here is that a number of factors have come together to make the Prime Minister's Office the centre of the system and far more powerful than the roots of the system. The system won't work that way and that simply has to change.

Bill Blaikie, New Democratic MP, 1979–Present

Power has been leaking out of Parliament for years and years in various ways, and we MPs are really fighting over the scraps. The fact is, the prime minister has most of what is left.

He makes all the appointments and everything runs through the Prime Minister's Office. So it's just human nature for people on the government side, in particular, to look over their shoulder and guard against making a move that would end their career. The prime minister has an awful lot of power.

Donald Savoie, Author of *Governing from the Centre*

The Canadian prime minister is an extremely powerful political person. In fact he holds in his hands all the key levers of political power. Indeed, if you compare his power to that of the president of the United States, the prime minister of Great Britain or the president of France, I would make the case that within the federal government he holds more power than his counterparts. Now, why do I say that? I say that for three or four reasons.

First, it seems he has the power in his hands to appoint everyone. He appoints Supreme Court judges, senators, Cabinet ministers, deputy ministers and so on. He holds in his hand the power to decide who makes it in the upper ranks and who does not. He sets the public policy agenda. No other person in this country can shape the public policy agenda to the same extent as the prime minister. He decides over the public purse. Key decisions of the budget are made in his office and by him. He is also the centre of media attention. If the media are going to focus on anybody in this country, it's on the prime minister. He dominates the media pages. So for those reasons I make the case that he is far more powerful than his counterparts elsewhere.

It's safe to say that the Supreme Court and the Senate no longer belong to Canadians. They belong to the prime minister. The prime minister will decide if somebody becomes a Supreme Court judge. It's the prime minister that will make a decision on who becomes a senator. I think 30 or 40 years ago it might have been appropriate, but today, as citizens become better engaged, better informed, they will want a say. It is their institution. It doesn't belong to a single politician. So there's cause for a great deal of concern.

Alan Tonks, Liberal MP, 2000–Present

I haven't been in the House as long as some Liberal backbenchers who feel the frustration regarding too much power in the Prime Minister's Office. My initial reaction is that it isn't the structure of the parliamentary system or the committee system that is at fault, but the House rules and procedures, as well as the culture itself. The feeling is that people are here for the right reasons, but they really feel frustrated because that isn't the message that's going out to the country.

Stanley Hartt, Former Chief of Staff to Prime Minister Brian Mulroney

The prime minister intentionally — when I say intentionally, I mean by the framers and makers of our Constitution — has these powers to appoint. Technically the power to appoint is Cabinet's power. Cabinet does ratify all the so-called prime ministerial appointments, none of these are individual calls. It is intentional that the prime minister has the power to make large numbers of so-called patronage appointments, that is, appointments to people whom the prime minister wants to reward for service in Parliament, service in the Cabinet, service in the public service or service to the political party. This is so that he can maintain the discipline on which our system depends. Remember, when he loses the support of the majority of the members of the House of Commons, visibly and externally as opposed to in their hearts, that's when he loses office and the government loses office.

Marlene Catterall, Liberal MP, 1997–Present; Current Government Whip

It is true that the power of appointment is one of the ways in which influence is exercised. I think that if you have public agencies, the government of the day obviously wants those public agencies to reflect the agenda that it is putting forward and trying to implement. That only makes sense to me. We've made sure that committees can review the appointments. There are a number of appointments on which there's always consultation with the opposition parties. And as a whip I can tell you that contrary to the sense that we're always fighting with each other — and that is what Question Period looks like — there is a tremendous amount of co-operation that goes on, on a daily basis.

When it comes to appointments — for instance, when it comes to me deciding who's going to be on what committees — I will talk to virtually all of my caucus colleagues. I will look at what they've done in the past, what committees they've served on, what they've said they want to do.

The power of appointment that the prime minister holds must be emphasized. The Bloc Québécois had some of their researchers determine how many appointments a prime minister has at his or her disposal. The number they came up with was close to 2,100 senior government appointments made by the prime minister alone. Rewarding the loyalty of those below him in his party is the main mechanism by which the prime minister's power is maintained and exerted.

Recall what veteran MP Patrick Boyer said in Chapter 1 and how it relates to the centralization of power:

> Every chair of a committee sees herself or himself as next becoming a junior Cabinet minister. Every junior Cabinet minister sees himself becoming a more senior Cabinet minister. And most senior Cabinet ministers aspire to become prime minister. So what we have going on in our Parliament is this wonderful game of political ambition that's motivating people every step of the way. They're learning how to hold their tongue — how to be polite and deferential to the one who can appoint them higher up. So they're not becoming critics.

Boyer is referring to the way loyalty is rewarded among politicians, and how the greasy pole of politics in the House of Commons works to stop MPs elected to the ruling party from holding the government to account or criticizing it. By controlling who sits at the top of government committees and deciding which MPs get into Cabinet, the prime minister's reach can be leveraged into the top ranks of the civil service, ambassadorships and the Senate. Kiss the prime minister's ring and your chances for promotion go up. Defy his will and your career path will be short.

The prime minister also has at his disposal the power to decide, unilaterally, when to hold federal elections. In so doing, he can control the tax and spending policies of the government to such an extent that he can pad his electoral chances by ensuring the election is called at the politically most advantageous time. In other words, he can ensure that money is being spent for the most visible and expedient political purposes right before an election is called. As you will see in Chapter 4, this was done in the 2000 election when $23 billion was restored to the health-care budget just weeks before the election was called. To top it off, the prime minister has the political power to veto his own party's MPs' plans to run in an election. He must by law sign their nomination papers and can punish them by not signing them if he so chooses.

With MPs looking to the prime minister to ensure their next promotion is on its way, what is Parliament's role in voting for these appointments and determining who occupies these important government positions? There is no role. Except for rubber-stamping appointments made by the prime minister, there is no parliamentary scrutiny of appointments — a frightening fact that few Canadians realize.

Through what are called "orders-in-council," not only does the prime minister appoint all his political underlings in Cabinet, he also appoints the head of state — the governor general — the head of the military and RCMP, all deputy ministers, the governor of the Bank of Canada, the head of the CBC, all senior foreign postings and all senators. And the levers of power do not stop there. The prime minister also appoints all judges on the Supreme Court (who interpret the Constitution on our behalf), plus all other federal court judges. As well, he designates the members of all Crown corporations, federal government commissions and boards. The fact is that MPs and Parliament are simply part of the patronage appointment merry-go-round.

Stanley Hartt, Former Chief of Staff to Prime Minister Brian Mulroney

Members of Parliament don't get to make the appointments; they are the objects of those appointments. In other words, they will either get appointments or not get them, depending on whether individual members vote the way they are meant to vote. But that's our system. Our system depends on MPs voting according to the mandate they receive from the voters and the internal democratic processes of their own political party.

The prime minister is then given prerogatives to use discipline which will keep the loyalty of his party members so that they stay in Parliament. For example, he can decide when the election is, unlike the American system, where you can predict the next 5,000 American elections just by using the calendar. In Canada that prerogative lies with the prime minister. Why does that lie with the prime minister? Because if he gets dissident members in his caucus objecting to stuff that he wants to do, he can say, "How would you like to run in an election? How would you like to defend your seat again? Do you think you'd win your seat tomorrow? I'm confident that I'd win mine. If you don't want an election tomorrow, stand up and vote the way I tell you to vote." His prerogatives are on purpose. They're part of our system to help him keep the discipline in his party so that he can keep his majority in government.

Peter MacKay, Progressive Conservative MP, 1997–Present

If members of Parliament are to be more relevant and play a more meaningful role in decision making, some power has to trickle down. That can only be demonstrated when the prime minister stops browbeating members of his own caucus, preventing them from speaking their minds and standing up on behalf of their constituents on very important issues.

Bill Blaikie, New Democratic MP, 1979–Present

Wouldn't it be a breath of fresh air if, in the case of public uproar, legislation could be defeated because members of Parliament say, "No, my constituents don't like that. And I don't like that. And I'm not voting for it"? I think people would drop dead in the streets, they'd be so surprised.

If the government always wins, if the government always gets its way, it starts to look like an elected dictatorship. That is how a lot of people feel about our current system. It is like a dictatorship in which one gets to choose another dictator every four years.

Marlene Catterall, Liberal MP 1997–Present; Current Government Whip

I've heard the suggestion that there is a concentration of power that has resulted in a benign, benevolent dictatorship. I personally don't think so. It may seem that decisions are made without consultation, but a great deal of discussion goes on before something comes to Parliament. It will often go on with opposition parties as well as among the Liberal members. Things are not a surprise when they come to Parliament.

The prime minister can say, "This is going to happen," and it will happen. How long does a leader remain a leader by doing that? You can't lead people where they're not ready to go, and if you're setting off in a direction and nobody's behind you, you aren't leader for very long. I think our system works well that way. Ultimately, though, it is the prime minister who is responsible. It is a minister who is responsible, and they have to make the tough decisions. Ministers have to listen to members of Parliament, as well as listen to Canadians. But they're the ones who are accountable in the end. Now, if you want to change that whole accountability relationship and say, "I'm accountable for my own actions. I have nothing to do with what the government does or what my party does in Parliament," then you're talking about anarchy, as far as I'm concerned.

Peter MacKay, **Progressive Conservative MP, 1997–Present**
It appears on the government side that there is really very little genuine interest in relinquishing some of the power possessed in the Prime Minister's Office and in the Privy Council Office. With the hepatitis C debate, many members of the Liberal Party did not support the government on the issue, but were forced to vote for a policy they did not believe in. The ethics counsellor was another classic case where Liberals had to vote against their own party's 1993 *Red Book* election promise to have the counsellor report directly to Parliament, not to the prime minister. I mean, Liberal members stood up in the House, ashen-faced, and were forced to vote against their own platform promise. It has to be completely humiliating for a member of Parliament to have to do that.

Back in the 1970s Prime Minister Pierre Trudeau said that MPs were nobodies 50 yards off Parliament Hill. Today the issue of prime ministerial control over the members of his or her own political party is a touchy one to discuss with any MP on the government side of the House of Commons. When I brought up the topic of parliamentary free votes in which each MP is able to vote independently, without regard to the party line, most MPs were uncomfortable, even defensive, with my questions. Some MPs were adamant that they do in fact vote as they choose, and when they had voted against their conscience from time to time, that was because they had already aired their views behind closed doors at caucus meetings — meetings not seen or heard by the public.

Indeed, many back-bench MPs on the government side claim caucus is where their influence rests. Many MPs made statements similar to what Liberal MP Paddy Tornsey said to our cameras:

The prime minister, as our leader, encourages a really full debate in caucus. If there is a policy that someone is trying to move forward and there are groups within caucus, or even two individuals, saying, "No, no, no, I don't like this at all," they hear all the problems. They'll say to the Cabinet ministers, "You don't move forward until you resolve these issues. We move forward as a group." At the end of the day there are probably some people that can't, that still would be out there. I've never found myself out there because I recognize you don't win every point. You don't win every battle. You work together, and as long as the goals and what the group is trying to achieve is basically on target, that's good. I guess those people vote against the government or stay away for the vote if they can't support the policy. But I've never found myself in that position.

Or what former Liberal MP Ted McWhinney stated:

Frankly, nobody's a "nobody" unless they give up. Within the caucus, if you know how to raise an issue properly, you can win. The thing you don't do in caucus is make 20-minute speeches. Three minutes is about the maximum tolerance level. You have got to explain complex issues in very clear language and you've got to keep coming back again and again and go directly to the minister.

This was not an uncommon point among our interviewees, but it made me wonder just how in-depth the debate in caucus can be when the tolerance of the MPs was a three-minute speech? How much insight and understanding can MPs have in these caucus debates? As well, from recent newspaper reports, I questioned just how open and free the debate was in caucus, and whether the prime minister was really open to dissent in his ranks. For instance, in January 2002 it was widely reported that Prime Minister Chrétien read the riot act to Toronto Liberal MP Carolyn Bennett for publicly questioning why the number of newly appointed women in his Cabinet shuffle was so small. Evidently the dressing down and screaming from the prime minister she had to endure in the next caucus meeting was very unfriendly and nearly brought her to tears in front of her colleagues. Clearly the prime minister's actions were meant to send a strong message to the rest of his caucus.

John Nunziata, Liberal MP, 1984–1996; Independent MP 1996–2000
Caucus meetings are nothing more than giant focus groups when MPs come to Ottawa. It's a bitch session for MPs. They can complain and they can squawk but ultimately the leader makes the decision. Decisions are taken in advance. I can't tell you the number of initiatives the government took without reference to the caucus when I was in the government caucus. MPs would read about these initiatives in the newspapers or see them on television even before there was any discussion whatsoever. So as far as influence is concerned, it's all phony influence.

Let's take the budget, for example. Government members see the budget for the first time when everyone else sees it, when Peter Mansbridge and Mike Duffy see it. That's the first time they see the budget, and in terms of having influence, they don't have any more influence than any other citizens' group that might bring forward their concerns. They can express their concerns at caucus but the government listens more to the opposition than they do to their own government members. They're very sensitive to the headlines every day and to what the opposition is saying.

Michael Harris, Journalist and Author
I don't think much has changed for backbenchers since Trudeau said MPs were nobodies 50 yards off Parliament Hill. I think that the back-bench MP who can't get on a committee, who can't become a parliamentary secretary, let alone end up in the Cabinet one day, is a person who is basically a pawn in the game of chess. He's pushed up and down the board according to the party whip, and his own views on matters are rarely if ever heard. So it's really a recipe for frustration to sit in the back bench for your career in Parliament.

As a journalist, what I've seen over the years I've been in the business is a gradual concentration away from the elected member, away from the minister, right up to the top level. I don't think the power is held in Cabinet. I think the power is held in the PMO, and that's not just a function of our federal politics. If you look at what's happening in Queen's Park, no minister of the Ontario government moves without approval through the premier's office. In fact, here in Ottawa someone like senior policy advisor Eddie Goldenberg has a lot more power than several Cabinet ministers. It's the people who make a full-time job out of the politics of public life rather than public administration who decide when elections are called and who will be the spokespeople on the really sensitive issues. The people who are closest to the seat of power enjoy the ear of the prime minister.

For example, when the original Donald Marshall story broke in 1983 and 1984, Marshall had been in prison for 11 years for something he hadn't done. It was under the jurisdiction of the Government of Nova Scotia, but I found it impossible to get an interview with the justice minister of the province because the people around him closed the door. The ordinary members of that legislature understood what a potentially explosive issue it was, but the response of the people in power was to control the information. MPs are powerless for a lot of reasons. One reason is they are not privy to the top-level information of their own government.

Brian Tobin, Former Liberal MP and Cabinet Minister

The opposition may say all the power is in the Prime Minister's Office, that there are unelected, faceless, unaccountable people in a dark backroom running the country. That's a great conspiracy theory, but it isn't the truth. There is a bias that there's some powerful handful of people, off in one of the buildings in Ottawa, that runs the whole country and the rest of us don't have a chance to participate. Anybody who believes that Cabinet operates completely disconnected from the power and the responsibility of caucus is making a very big mistake.

The prime minister is successful because the prime minister delegates. I have the same opportunity as anybody else in Cabinet or caucus to be heard. The mark of leadership is the capacity to keep the troops together in the tent, to acknowledge and encourage differences of opinion and then to build consensus. Jean Chrétien recognizes that he can't do it all alone. He's got a lot of bright and energetic and ambitious people around him.

There is a greater dispersal of political power in this country today, more than ever before.

John Nunziata, Liberal MP, 1984–1996; Independent MP 1996–2000
When you're on the government side, power is concentrated in the hands of half a dozen people, half of whom are not elected. All the power rests with the Prime Minister's Office and everything else is window-dressing. Pierre Trudeau referred to MPs as nobodies 50 yards off the Hill and Mr. Chrétien has turned MPs into nobodies — even *his* MPs — right on the floor of the House of Commons.

In the 1997 election 62 percent of those who voted, voted against the Liberals. So Jean Chrétien, with 38 percent of the popular vote, had 100 percent of the power. That's hardly an expression of the will of the people. Until we change the power structure in Ottawa, until we take power away from the non-elected people in the Prime Minister's Office, we will continue to have a system that's very severely flawed, undemocratic and dictatorial.

Reg Alcock, Liberal MP, 1993–Present
The House of Commons actually has enormous authority, but at certain key points that authority is controlled by one person or elites. Senior mandarins and senior folks in some of the interest groups that circle around Ottawa exert an enormous amount of control, and I think a very unhealthy amount of control. An awful lot of control has been centralized in the higher levels of the bureaucracy and in the Prime Minister's Office. We need to separate that control to allow the House to function as a body to demand accountability from the government. This won't happen quickly, however, because it's good to be the king.

How potent the central power in Ottawa is depends on whom you listen to. Compare the statements made by Liberal member Reg Alcock and former Liberal MP John Nunziata with the comments of Brian Tobin, Chrétien's former minister of industry. Those inside Cabinet tend to defend the system a lot more vigorously than those outside it.

The existence of centralized power is certain. Nearly everyone refers to it as a natural reality.

"Benign dictatorship" or "semi-dictatorship" are two of the most commonly used descriptors. *Globe and Mail* columnist Jeffrey Simpson called his most recent book, on the subject of the centralization of government power, *The Friendly Dictatorship*. The word "dictatorship" flows off people's lips so readily when they refer to the prime minister that it is starting to permeate the public's view of its government. This cannot be a good thing.

But what, and who, are these central agencies that evidently rule our lives?

Donald Savoie, Author of *Governing from the Centre*

Central agencies are there for a single purpose: to assist the prime minister in running the government. The Privy Council Office is his department. It has no programs. It's not distorted in its views. It focuses exclusively on the needs of the prime minister, shapes what goes into Cabinet, determines what's decided in Cabinet, dictates those decisions and sends them to all departments. It is the focal point of decisions. The Prime Minister's Office and the Privy Council Office are there to advise the prime minister in terms of appointments. They decide who makes it into the Senate.

Central agencies are there to assist the PM in all of his functions. The Department of Finance has a minister, as well as a special relationship with the prime minister because he dominates the budget process. Key decisions fall in his hands, so the Department of Finance is there to advise him. So central agencies — and there are three or four of them that are well staffed by the most senior and competent public servants — are there to assist the PM. This increases his levers of power.

Joe Clark, **Progressive Conservative Leader and Former Prime Minister**

Theoretically the Prime Minister's Office is composed of people who are there to help a prime minister carry out his or her functions. In fact they've become instruments of control. They want to set the agenda, which is natural enough. There's nothing wrong with them wanting to set an agenda or wanting to bring coherence to a government program. What's wrong is that there is so little control over them by anybody outside the prime minister's direct entourage. In the United States the Senate has clear powers and the Congress has clear powers. The president is an immensely powerful office in the United States, but there are also clear constitutional limits on it. Here in Canada there are very few that can be made effective.

Harry Swain, **Deputy Minister of Industry, 1992–1995**

The Prime Minister's Office, some have said, is an extension of a prime minister who is a four-year dictator. That's an extreme view held by some friends of mine. I wouldn't go that far. But it is certainly true, in our system a prime minister wields a great deal of power, mostly through powers that are not written down. It's kind of interesting, but nowhere in the Constitution are the words "prime minister" or "Cabinet" even mentioned. But the prime minister appoints all members of Cabinet. He decides what their jobs will be and how broad their powers will be. He appoints all deputy ministers. Well, right there, you sure got everybody's attention. The people who work closely with him in the Prime Minister's Office, his political wing, are few in number, but generally pretty high in quality and guile. They can wield an enormous amount of power, if they want to.

I do recall one time being instructed to give a press conference by a senior member of the Prime Minister's Office. The normal question from PMO is, "You did what? Why?" And then you have a chance to explain. A lot of central agency work, both political and bureaucratic, has an emergency quality to it. "Stamping out fires" is one way of putting it. "Dealing with the urgent matters of the day" is another. Often these transcend the powers or interests of a particular department. The central agencies, which can bring together several different organs in government, play quite an important role there, and the PMO is among them.

Keith Martin, Reform and Canadian Alliance MP, 1993–Present

The small group of people who run Parliament are usually advisors to the leadership. They are advisors to the prime minister who are appointed by the prime minister, who gives them power to advise him on issues. And through that they also have the power to go to Cabinet and to MPs and say, "This is what you do."

I tried valiantly to have members of the current Prime Minister's Office agree to on-camera TV interviews, to no avail. Not even a courteous letter of refusal. Nothing. I can only assume the same thing would have happened if I tried to get someone from the Mulroney PMO to speak to me back when he was in power.

During my various requests for interviews with the upper echelons of the government, I witnessed a media pecking order in Ottawa. There seemed to be a very managed arrangement between the media and the government. I judged by my discussions with various parliamentary journalists that getting access to high-ranking government officials is always a difficult task. However, it appeared doubly difficult for those who were not part of the traditional media game in Ottawa, like myself.

Thankfully, however, I have spoken to several high-ranking members of former prime minister Brian Mulroney's office, both on the record and off. With time, people beyond the reach of power seem to lose their fear of telling it like it is.

Although you have read a few of his quotes already, I want to point directly to one of my favourite interviewees, Stanley Hartt, former deputy minister of finance (1985–89) and former chief of staff in the Mulroney PMO (1990–92). Stanley Hartt's candid responses regarding how the Prime Minister's Office actually operates shed substantial light into dark corners. He seemed to enjoy the tough questions and provided his unsettling answers with a rare lucidity. I must admit I didn't always like what I heard, but Hartt, to his credit, portrayed the clearest reflection of how things really work in the Prime Minister's Office and how the prime minister exercises his unprecedented power.

Stanley Hartt, Former Chief of Staff to Prime Minister Brian Mulroney

The PMO has an almost impossible job. It's supposed to help the prime minister develop policy that is consistent with his platform. It's supposed to attend to his travel, speaking and schedule needs. It's supposed to worry about image, press and communications. And it's got a tiny staff to do all that. It does have the benefit of working with the Privy Council Office on policy matters. But what I found was there's an awful lot to do with a very few people.

I think it's very easy to blame the Prime Minister's Office because the PMO is almost partly there to be blamed. You don't want to stand up and say the prime minister is mean. So you say the Prime Minister's Office is mean, they're tough, they're not respectful of democratic rights. It's very easy to pick the PMO as the whipping boy. The PMO staff doesn't wield any power. The distance is given to them expressly and by delegation from the prime minister himself. The second he wants them to stop doing anything that they're doing, he says so and they stop.

I wouldn't say it was fun working in the Prime Minister's Office. I would say it was the hardest job I'd ever had. It was harder than being a lawyer with a very complex corporate and securities practice. It was harder than running a huge bankrupt real estate and retail company with 110,000 employees and getting them out of bankruptcy. It was harder than dreaming up brilliant investment and banking ideas, which I do now for a vast variety of companies. It was the hardest thing I ever did by far, way harder than being deputy minister of finance. There are so many pressures on you from so many different directions. Your reaction to them had to be so instantaneous, and you had so few allies that you could count on, that it was very difficult.

There are certain talents that you have to have. First of all, you have to understand the political process. Second, it helps in the Prime Minister's Office if you have a strong tie to or tradition with the ruling political party. I realize that I didn't have particularly strong ties with the party, but that does help. It helps to know the MPs personally from other activities that you've been engaged in. So that when you go to talk to them you're not necessarily there as the threatening guy from the

PMO. You're just a friend who wants to help the party succeed, stay in office and prosper.

Donald Savoie, **Author of** *Governing from the Centre*

If power is concentrated around the centre, and the prime minister can naturally only handle four or five pet projects or issues at a time, the other issues and policies are left at bay. The prime minister will focus on only certain key files — for example, Pierre Trudeau and the Constitution, Brian Mulroney and free trade, Jean Chrétien and the deficit situation and the foundation for innovation. These are the files that each prime minister will carefully embrace and work on.

The rest of the system is expected not to make waves — to ride the issues out without making any big mistakes and ensure there are no scandals in the media. The prime minister will tell his ministers and deputy ministers, whom he appoints, "Look, we're focusing on those four or five key priorities. Your job is to make sure we don't rock the boat, that things go smoothly — and I don't want your name on the front page of *The Globe and Mail* saying something is screwed up."

Stanley Hartt, **Former Chief of Staff to Prime Minister Brian Mulroney**

I think the prime minister's personal role is totally leadership driven. His staff has to pay attention to stamping out fires. That's a lot of what we did. I found that, personally, when I got there I was distracted by the fact that we had emergency after emergency. I don't know if people will remember, but we had a rumour that turned out to be true, that a Chilean terrorist had put cyanide in our grapes. We had to recall all the grapes on every grocery shelf in Canada and examine them, and we found two that indeed had cyanide in them — not at levels that would have hurt anybody, but we couldn't take that chance.

Then we had a Lebanese terrorist hijack a bus in Montreal, drive it to Parliament Hill with 11 people on it and threaten to blow it up. We had to surround Parliament Hill with sharpshooters and talk him out of the bus — and on and on and on. And yes, I did have the impression that we were distracted from helping the prime minister build a platform of legislative ideas that was consistent with his platform, would appeal to the public and keep his popularity high.

The Prime Minster's Office seems to wield power not because they arrogate to themselves the chance to do this or the need to do that but because the power comes from our structure. It comes from the power the prime minister himself or herself wields. The prime minister is powerful in our system because the prime minister is by definition a leader of the party that has the most seats in Parliament.

Traditionally the prime minister is not supposed to be all powerful, but rather "first among equals," as Walter Bagehot stated in writings on the British Parliament. The Cabinet is supposed to be very powerful and is the place where other potential prime ministers supposedly can hone their skills and knowledge of governing. The Canadian Constitution is clear on this subject. There is actually no provision for the position of prime minister in our Constitution. It says little about how a prime minister is chosen. It simply states that the government will be formed from the majority members of the House of Commons. In our recent history the political parties have taken over the task of choosing who will lead each political party. Then, once elected to government, the party with the most seats sees to it that its leader is given the title of prime minister. The prime minister is then granted the power to choose a Cabinet.

The hard-to-ignore question is, where is Cabinet in the power hierarchy today? Remember, along with the prime minister, the Cabinet is the other arm of government that makes up what is called the executive branch. Cabinet is supposed to have clout, influence and power.

As long-time federal Cabinet minister John Crosbie said in a TV interview several years ago, things have changed:

It's really quite humorous to see how it operates. The prime minister has a staff whose job it is to make sure that he can't get blamed for anything. If anything bad happens, it's the fault of one of those turkeys in the Cabinet. They now regard the leader as sacrosanct. He's not the first among equals anymore. The prime minister is a "supreme being" and the Cabinet ministers are peasants down below and lucky to survive.

Perhaps the "first among equals" concept has become more like "first me, then you, if you stay loyal to me and don't question my authority."

Donald Savoie, **Author of** *Governing from the Centre*

In many ways the prime minister is his own boss. It's true that every four years he has to face the Canadian people, but if he or she decides not to run for re-election, then there's very little check in terms of political power.

In theory the Cabinet should make up the executive, as the official decision- and policy-making body of the Government of Canada. In practice it doesn't quite work like that. The prime minister chairs all Cabinet meetings and the prime minister will dictate at the end. If the consensus goes his way, there's no problem. If it doesn't go his way, he can hold it up. He can say, "We'll come back to it in a month." So Cabinet has become more or less policy advisors, much like his staff. A minister of this government observed that it's no longer a decision-making body, that Cabinet has become a focus group. I think that defines the problem.

Keith Martin, **Reform and Canadian Alliance MP, 1993–Present**

Most Cabinet ministers have very little power, contrary to popular belief. They themselves have been told what to say and what to do. Their deputy ministers are appointed by the Prime Minister's Office, not by themselves. So unfortunately we have a situation where Cabinet ministers, many of whom are competent and intelligent, are forced to do as they are told. Now, if a minister, no differently from a back-bench MP, were to say, "No, I'm not going to do that," they're out of a job. So as an MP you have to make a decision, I think. Do you want to fight for the right thing? Do you want to stand up and take chances? Do you want to lead from the front? Or do you want to play the game? And some would argue that if you play the game, you get to the top, you get into a position of influence. But those who get to that position of so-called influence, that Holy Grail of positions — Cabinet — often find that they are less powerful than they used to be as back-bench MPs because they have very little opportunity to innovate. Right now in Parliament we are seeing the death of innovation.

Brian Tobin, Former Liberal MP and Cabinet Minister

That's just nonsense. This prime minister is successful because this prime minister delegates. Anybody who believes that Minister of Finance Paul Martin is not playing a substantial and important role in shaping the finance policy, fiscal and monetary policy, of Canada is dreaming in Technicolor. Anybody who believes that I'm standing still here over at Industry Canada and not driving hard on an agenda for innovation, for creating the most connected and smartest country we can, is dreaming in Technicolor.

Today ministers are very aware, and the prime minister's very aware, of what is being said in the various regional caucuses across the country, what's being said in the national caucus and what's happening in the standing committees of the House of Commons. While Cabinet ultimately gets to make the call, every member of Cabinet has got their finger on the pulse of a great many institutions; parliamentary institutions, caucus institutions and economic institutions which all bear on judgments in policy.

Stanley Hartt, Former Chief of Staff to Prime Minister Brian Mulroney

There were Cabinet ministers and there were Cabinet ministers. The leading Cabinet ministers — those that ran the central agencies, like Deputy Prime Minister Don Mazankowski or the minister of finance, Michael Wilson — were extremely powerful in my day. All Cabinets have to work on the basis that the minister of finance has a veto at the Cabinet table because otherwise the spenders will have him every time. His fiscal framework, his budget, will just be blown to smithereens within days of its announcement in the House. So there are some very powerful Cabinet ministers. There are other ministers, not just with lesser portfolios, but who, by their personality, don't command the respect and loyalty of their colleagues to the same degree. They don't have the same control of the reins of power as the central agencies have. Those ministers may often have to fight for visibility.

I have come to the conclusion that one of the fundamental reasons we have seen such a remarkable rise of centralized power in

Canada is that many of us have simply forgotten, or were never taught, the differences between what the executive of government is and what the legislature is. This is a key issue that all Canadians must grasp if we are to govern ourselves better. Again, the executive is the prime minister and the Cabinet. Parliament, made up of the House of Commons and the Senate, is our national legislature. Parliament is there to ensure that the executive is in check, to pass our laws and to hold the government accountable. The executive is clearly getting the upper hand over Parliament.

Many Canadians criticize our American neighbours for their lack of knowledge on world issues and their isolationist outlook. However, if there is one thing they know that we Canadians don't, it is the difference between the legislature and the executive. It has been drummed into their heads since grade school: the executive is the president and his appointed but congressionally approved Cabinet; the legislature is Congress, the elected members of the U.S. Senate and the House of Representatives. I am always impressed by how the average citizen in the U.S. understands the "checks and balances" system of government, where the elected legislature checks the power of the unelected executive. The president does not move on any issue without persuading the Senate and the House of Representatives to vote with him. Nothing is railroaded through Congress.

It's interesting how we Canadians choose our executives in the Cabinet. They are selected from a pool of elected MPs in the governing party. Are these MPs good managers? Are they talented in dealing with people, dealing with billion-dollar budgets, understanding national and international issues or providing a vision for their departments? Let's hope so. But perhaps they are only really good at getting elected and being loyal to the prime minister. Or maybe the MP is not capable at all, but represents a province or riding that the prime minister wants to ensure is seen in Cabinet.

As the prime minister is able to select members of his Cabinet only from the pool of elected people in his caucus, it is questionable whether Canadians are getting the best people to run the country. Our system of government rewards MPs for their political skills and offers small incentive to professionals and accomplished specialists to enter politics.

Ted McWhinney, Liberal MP, 1993–2000

Canadians mix up the executive and the legislature, and I'm not sure it's very healthy to mix them these days. The qualities required to get elected to office as a member of Parliament are not necessarily the qualities to be a good executive (prime minister or Cabinet minister), and certainly the reverse is true. Correspondingly, since our members of Parliament are already into this double function (of having to get elected as well as being an executive in the Canadian government), I don't think they're able to spend the time necessary in the legislative process.

I've seen many excellent people in the Canadian business community and labour community who would be very good members of a Cabinet, but couldn't possibly be elected in Canada. They don't have the personality, the patience or the discipline to go about being elected. So I think the executive talent available in Canada's Parliament is very much weaker than in the United States.

The case of General McNaughton is the best example. Poor General McNaughton was commander of the Canadian Forces in World War II, and Mackenzie King wanted him in the Cabinet. He tried twice to find him a safe seat, but he was beaten each time. He was totally hopeless as a communicator, but in terms of the direct conversational exchanges with the prime minister or others as commander-in-chief, he was excellent.

The executive in the United States is selected through its elected Congress for totally different reasons. You select them for their specialist confidence or their overall capacities. I couldn't have seen Colin Powell being elected, for example, as a senator or a congressman, or having the patience to put up with it, but I think he's going to be a great secretary of state.

The only way we can bring these sorts of quality people into our Canadian system is to create a by-election. The prime minister gets one of his MPs to retire, puts them in our appointed Senate — which is a joke by comparison with the American Senate — and selects somebody to run for the empty seat.

The hazard in our system is as follows: if everyone who is elected is looking to become a member of the Cabinet, and hence an executive of government, then who is overseeing the executive? All the evidence thus far clearly points to the fact that Parliament is not overseeing the Cabinet ministers, while the prime minister holds an immense amount of power over his executive.

One might argue that the strength of the Prime Minister's Office and the Privy Council Office is simply a symptom of our weak legislatures. Central agencies have become necessary to manage the massive size and scope of our government, while Parliament has become weak in trying to scrutinize the government's actions. There simply are not enough scrutinizing MP eyes doing the job.

So what? Who cares if we have what people are calling a four-year dictatorship? We still can get up in the morning, have a decent standard of living, and the country still runs. We can boot the prime minister out every four years if we choose. What are the threats and consequences of having a prime minister with so much power over the country?

Anne Cools, Liberal Senator, 1984–Present

We have to be mindful of governance, as opposed to government. The governance of a nation is an extremely important function. We also have to remember that most human beings are pretty good people. But we cannot exist in a system where you depend on the extremely virtuous because the extremely virtuous are few and far between.

Donald Savoie, Author of *Governing from the Centre*

Since power is so concentrated, it enables the prime minister and his key advisors to turn around and make a decision fairly quickly. They don't have to worry about Congress. They don't have to worry about other forces inside. The downside, of course, is that because power is concentrated and because they control so much, there are a number of issues and errors that somehow do not surface. Canadians don't know what is happening on the inside. Hence it cuts both ways. On the one hand they're able to turn around decisions very quickly, and on the other hand it enables the prime minister to camouflage a number of issues that he doesn't want to see surface.

We're still able to pass judgment on the prime minister every four years. The problem is that to do that properly we need opposition parties that can become viable alternatives to the sitting government. We don't have that at the moment. So there is a great deal of concern.

Anne Cools, Liberal Senator, 1984–Present

Remember what Lord Acton said: "Absolute power corrupts absolutely." Parliament and the system of governance are supposed to understand that human beings with absolute power, or governors with unbridled power, invariably will abuse it. The business of Parliament is to make sure that power is always exercised very properly and very orderly on behalf of the citizens of the land.

However, if you were to look at the history of Parliament, and the history of the development of responsible government, it was all about wrestling power away from non-responsible, non-elected bodies — kings, usually. Now we see the situation ticking, slowly, but certainly and surely, back to something akin to the old system.

Donald Savoie, Author of *Governing from the Centre*

When power is so centralized, the implications are clear. Canadians do not understand how the process works. It's a hidden power. A lot of the decisions are made by a few key advisors and policy makers. Canadians are, for the most part, on the outside looking in. They don't have a sense of ownership. They don't understand the process. Parliament still sits, Question Period still exists and elections are still held. Canadians are moving away from having a sense of ownership in their government. In my mind that is serious.

Joe Clark, Progressive Conservative Leader and Former Prime Minister

I think it's broadly agreed that we need to restore the power of Parliament. The world's changed and the capacity of governments of any stripe to control media, to control events, to control parliaments has increased remarkably. Yet the prime minister of Canada has more power in Canada than the prime minister of the U.K. has in the U.K. He has certainly more power in his country than the president of the United States has in his. That has always been the case in the system, but recent changes have made that even more emphatic and, I think, dangerous in a country like this.

It's dangerous for two reasons. Firstly, it leads to a concentration of power in a government and an increasing isolation of government. It is true that power corrupts, and now it is more possible for a majority government of any political orientation to operate without constraint in the House of Commons than it was prior to this time. Secondly, the concentration of power reduces the variety of views that affect public policy in Canada.

Keith Martin, Reform and Canadian Alliance MP, 1993–Present

To voters it means that they have a group of people they didn't elect, whom they don't know and who have power directly from the prime minister, making decisions on the big policy issues of the country and determining where the country is going. That little group tells the Cabinet what to do, what to say, where to go and how to do it.

Basically what we have done is taken the Westminster system, bastardized it and turned it into a semi-dictatorship. The voter does matter, but the only time that we can truly exercise our democratic rights as members of the public is once every four or five years during an election. Between elections we have that unelected, unaccountable system, that pseudo-democracy, that dictatorship.

Bill Blaikie, New Democratic MP, 1979–Present

This is the larger democratic issue that parliamentary reform needs to tackle if it is really going to get to the root of the frustration that members of Parliament and the public feel about politics.

We need reform inside the House of Commons to redistribute power. This sense of powerlessness that members of Parliament have is related not just to the fact that they themselves have so little power, but also to the fact that Parliament itself has too little power because of the way it has been abdicated.

Reg Alcock, **Liberal MP, 1993–Present**

I chair this roundtable and at the roundtable we have some of the most senior analysts and mandarins in Ottawa, retired deputy ministers and such, who are very experienced. I was listening to two of them talking and making interventions at the table and one said that "the House of Commons is irrelevant." I thought, wait a second, it's easy to make fun of politicians because nobody likes politicians. But if we take out the word "politician" and put the word "citizen" in, to say that "the House of Commons is irrelevant" is such a shocking thing that surely we have to fix it.

Anne Cools, **Liberal Senator, 1984–Present**

I've made it my business to study this institution of Parliament because I love it and I believe in it. It took about 1,000 years to get certain powers away from the king. And supposedly they were to come to Parliament. But it took about 50 years to give those powers back to a prime minister. I sincerely believe that that is the case here in Canada.

This is a social and political question that is commanding study and demanding examination — the total buildup and accumulation of power. It's not only in the prime minister's hands, but in the Prime Minister's Office's hands. You now have a situation in this country where the executive, meaning the Cabinet, exercises the king's powers, the governor general's powers, the Senate's powers, the House of Commons's powers. I think that we should always be diligent about the accumulation of so many powers in so few hands. It worries me.

There is a need for change, and certainly an appetite for one. Giving up power while holding on to it is easier said than done. What are the obstacles to giving our Parliament, and by inference, citizens, a voice again in government?

I spoke to various interviewees about what has to happen for power to revert back from the centre, and particularly from the prime minister, to the legislature.

Peter Dobell, Director, The Parliamentary Centre

There are MPs who talk quite a lot about unhappiness with the system. But they don't do anything because you can't easily organize change. How would they do it? So the problem is they've got this real distress. But the power to change requires a majority of members and all parties agreeing. If you can't get all of those people together, you aren't going to get change.

Unless the system improves, our members of Parliament really won't feel as though they are making a contribution. They'll continue to be frustrated. This current Parliament is particularly feeling frustrated because they had a relatively small turnover. Almost 85 percent of the members have been here for one or two or three previous Parliaments, so they know what the problems are.

Reg Alcock, Liberal MP, 1993–Present

This is a change that has to happen on behalf of all of us, but it's going to threaten the system, the bureaucrats, and it's going to threaten those people who hold power right now. It's a process of those who have power giving it up and people just don't do that easily. There are very few examples, of which I can name two: Czech Republic president Vaclav Havel and José Figueras in Costa Rica. Other than that it's hard to identify political leaders who have voluntarily given up power, and that's my argument with Prime Minister Jean Chrétien. I think Chrétien's the guy to lead it, despite all of the battles he gets into.

I don't mean to be too flippant about this, but people suggested that the prime minister should instruct us to do parliamentary reform, but I keep saying no to the prime minister and my colleagues. It is the House of Commons which exercises the rights and responsibilities of citizens. The House needs to assert that responsibility, not go, cap in hand, begging to the prime minister for it. My challenge to the prime minister, publicly and privately, is to get into it with us, as an equal.

Bill Blaikie, New Democratic MP, 1979–Present

We need to transfer some of the power now concentrated in the Prime Minister's Office to ordinary members on both sides of the House in order to free them from the various structures that prevent them from having the kind of say that constituents would like them to have. We are mainly talking about freeing up government backbenchers because opposition MPs are already free to criticize the government. We want government back-benchers to be less constrained by the kind of party discipline that has made the Canadian parliamentary system so rigid.

Joe Clark, Progressive Conservative Leader and Former Prime Minister
A lot of people worry about chaos developing if there were more power to individual members of Parliament, but I don't worry about that at all. In fact, I'd go a lot farther than many other people. I would put much more power to initiate legislation in the hands of all party committees of the House. I think that on issues like the environment, like Indian affairs, you're likely to get more imagination out of a group of elected parliamentarians working together than you do out of the present system, in which these issues get treated as having a lower level of importance than budgets and other questions.

Now, we don't want to go to the American system because our own provides a means of control. That control comes down to accountability to Parliament, by being forced to answer questions in the House and going before a parliamentary committee to defend your estimates. I am the last prime minister — and I was the first — who ever took his own spending estimates to a committee and defended them before the Parliament of Canada, as other ministers should do. That's now unthinkable, but I'd do it again because I think that it is symbolically an indication of who's in charge: the members of Parliament and, through them, the people.

It would be a pipe dream to think that change is going to be initiated by the people who benefit now from the status quo. What I think is going to have to happen is a real demonstration in Parliament that the public won't put up with the status quo. I think there's increasing evidence that members of Parliament won't, and I think there are enough members of Parliament, in all parties, that favour change that puts more power in the hands of Parliament and less in the hands of government.

Donald Savoie, **Author of** *Governing from the Centre*

Is there anything that we can do about it? I think the solution lies in all of us. It lies in Canadians. We have to engage. We have to become empowered. Nobody's going to do it for us. The more citizens learn about how government works, the more they'll be able to articulate what they want and how changes should be made.

Peter Dobell, **Director, The Parliamentary Centre**

I'm persuaded that ultimately there has to be a change that is agreed upon by most of the MPs themselves. The prime minister doesn't have to lead the change, but he certainly has to agree. Parliamentary reform can come directly down from the prime minister or it can come from a slightly lower level, say the House leader of the ruling government party. But it must have not only the prime minister's approval; it must have the approval of the other parties.

I don't think change is going to happen in the next year or so. But it's quite possible that when a new prime minister comes in it might.

We need improvement. Citizens need their votes to be better articulated through the MPs we elect. We need parliamentarians to think for themselves and vote with their minds and their consciences, and to actually have some effect. We have a system in which change needs to be made by the very people who have a vested interest in not making change, the politicians. To get the MPs back into the loop of our national debate, we must depend on the prime minister to give up the power he now holds. If history is any indication, this will not happen easily.

Thankfully, on top of the vote we cast every four years, there are a few other accountability mechanisms that constrict the power of the federal government, and in particular the prime minister's actions. The provincial premiers have tried to assert their powers against the federal government, with a great deal of success. However, there is a troubling trend on the horizon of the federal government's relations with the provinces. It comes cloaked in the veil of an innocuous word: co-operation.

CHAPTER 4

The Provinces:

The Hope or the Faltering Prospect for Accountability in the Federal Government?

While discussing the issue of how centralized power has come about in Canada, journalist Michael Harris said:

> As a journalist, what I've seen over the years I've been in the business is a gradual concentration away from the elected MP, away from the minister, right up to the top level. I don't think the power is held in Cabinet. I think the power is held in the Prime Minister's Office, and that's not just a function of our federal politics. If you look at what's happening in Queen's Park, no minister of the Ontario government moves without approval through the premier's office.

Harris points to a troubling trend in federal and provincial politics. David Crombie, a former federal Cabinet minister and former mayor of Toronto, has noted a similar trend:

The first ministers of Canada basically run this country. And even there, it's a small number of first ministers. We have far more centralization of power than the U.S. has at that level. At the federal and provincial levels of government, the political party system increasingly delivers power to the Cabinet and, even more so, to the office of the prime minister or the office of the premier. Therefore we can have members of Parliament or members of provincial legislative assemblies who have no idea what's happening in the government because they're less and less connected to it.

Our interviews revealed that, with the premiers and the prime minister now running the political show, a new breed of decision making is taking place. Decisions have shifted from the elected MPs and members of provincial legislatures to the party leaders, and the result is something called "executive federalism." Executive federalism simply means that first ministers — the premiers and the prime minister — make many of the key decisions that affect Canadians' lives without the full participation of their legislatures and without the probing questions of opposition parties.

Executive federalism is not a bad thing per se, as it is one of the few ways in which the federal government is kept in check. Unlike ordinary Canadians, the premiers often have the power to hold the federal government to its word.

But as we conducted our interviews, I began to realize that most Canadians, and even many politicians and political watchers, take it for granted that executive federalism just happens. Little evidence was ever offered to prove its legitimacy. Before I present the interviews we conducted on this point, let's step back to Confederation and ask what the term "federalism" really means.

In grade school, and sadly even in university, my eyes used to glaze over whenever a teacher would use the word federalism. At its mere utterance I would start snoozing. I avoided any essay topic related to this soporific subject. Surely part of the blame for my lack of interest was my teachers' collective inability to spell out just how significant federalism was to how the country works. In recent years, through working on these documentary film interviews, I began to realize the true meaning of federalism and to appreciate just how bastardized Canada's federal state has become.

A federal system of government simply means that at least two levels of government run the affairs of the state. But it seems most Canadians forget why our Constitution was written in the first place. The idea was to bring the founding provincial partners together to join in a "confederation," a federal state where power between the provinces and the federal government would be split and in some cases shared. Each level of government would have specific duties to perform on behalf of their citizens, based on the deal each had signed to form the federal government and create the Constitution it would be governed by.

The reason our forefathers sought this sort of arrangement was that they had learned the most important lesson in political history: that political power must be dispersed and restrained, not centralized. History has long shown that those with political power inevitably abuse it. From Caligula to Joseph Stalin, history is full of tyrants, kings and dictators who have abused their power over their citizens. So to avoid a concentration of power, our wise forefathers divided power between two levels of government. But their good intentions are being forgotten today and our elected officials are becoming the pawns of a powerful few.

The following excerpt comes from a lengthy interview with Brian Kelcey, a self-described "spin-doctor" who worked in intergovernmental affairs for the Ontario government. At a first ministers' conference he witnessed how billion-dollar decisions that affect us all are made.

Brian Kelcey, Former Communications Officer, Government of Ontario

A first ministers' meeting is a formal meeting between the premiers of the various provinces and the prime minister during which they attempt to resolve issues of conflict. There is a common misconception that first ministers' meetings take place regularly. Although there are regular meetings of provincial and federal ministers, first ministers' meetings are extremely rare. They happen only when the prime minister decides that there is something on his political agenda that he believes he can persuade all of the provincial premiers to agree to.

The key condition for these meetings is that they are under the control of the prime minister. The premiers may ask for first ministers' meetings on all sorts of subjects, but until the prime minister agrees and says, "These are the conditions and the issues that you're free to discuss at a table with me on a particular day," the meeting will not happen.

As a press secretary with the Ontario delegation, I attended a first ministers' meeting in September 2000. Essentially the prime minister wanted to cover his vulnerability on health care because the provinces had been demanding or asking the federal government to reinstate former levels of provincial health-care funding. The prime minister was politically motivated to get this done (due to the coming election) and the stakes of this meeting were very high. We are talking about billions of dollars changing hands from the federal government back into the coffers of the provinces.

The Ontario government knew clearly what they wanted from the meeting: their demand to Ottawa for a return of federal funding on health care to the level that existed in 1995 had been an Ontario Tory campaign promise during the 1999 provincial election. So we had a very clear mandate to ask for what we were asking for. On the other hand, what our demand actually translated into in terms of the real mechanics of government, what that meant for ordinary people, depended entirely on the federal offer, and that only appeared the morning of the day the meeting started.

The process of making decisions about billions of dollars at these meetings is bizarre to me. On one hand, you see that the premiers, as individuals and as a group, and the prime minister are much smarter and much shrewder than I think a lot of the public gives them credit for. But on the other hand, what was really unusual about the meeting was that the provinces had been asking the prime minister for a proposal to fund health care for several months. Yet they didn't see the actual multibillion-dollar federal proposal they were supposed to make a decision on until the moment they arrived on September 11, 2000. In this case it was a $23-billion deal affecting the future of health care in this country, and the provinces were supposed to make a decision on the federal government's offer within five or six hours of the beginning of that meeting.

I don't think anybody would want to make a decision about $23 billion on an issue that is as important as health care within a few hours. Ontario had been asking for details for months from the federal government to make sure that we could discuss this thing intelligently and work out all the details. But frankly, the way the process worked, which was in large part under the control of the federal government, we had no choice but to sit at that table on their timetable and work everything out. And we had to do it within a few hours with information that the premier and our government had only received moments before.

In situations like the first ministers' meeting, you have only hours to make a decision worth billions of dollars. That kind of time constraint doesn't make for great working conditions. Essentially you have support staff, I think there were seven or eight of us from Ontario, crammed into a couple of cubicles. Smaller provinces or territories got one cubicle. If you leaned the wrong way in a cubicle, you would find yourself in Nunavut or Manitoba. Within that space you have a laptop and maybe a speakerphone to work with. From the conference room where the premiers and the prime minister are meeting, you either get premiers wandering down with information about what they think the deal looks like or you will get an occasional note from inside the meeting. And on the basis of that information alone you must figure out, "Is this something that solves the problems we are looking at?" There is a great deal of confusion, even within the negotiating process, as to what the federal offer means because you haven't had the advance time to work out what it is that's sitting on the table.

The dynamic of these meetings is one of junior grade geopolitics, in the sense that alliances are important. The whole idea is to have consensus between premiers. You develop networks of friends and enemies. You have better relationships with some provinces than with others. Those relationships develop just as much on the basis of personality or political perception or partisanship as they do on the basis of whether you have a common interest at the meeting. It's a very chaotic dynamic — and a very chaotic process to work in.

The other agenda item at the September 2000 meeting was the so-called National Children's Agenda. In terms of the order of priorities, to the premiers it was very important, but it was still secondary to the health-care problem that had been on their agenda for a year or so. Because we didn't hear the federal offer on health care until that very morning, we couldn't map out what that meant for the National Children's Agenda. By the middle of the day I was speaking to reporters who didn't know whether the roughly $2 billion the feds were putting toward the National Children's Agenda was in their offer for the Canada Health and Social Transfer (CHST) or in addition to the $23 billion.

There was a press conference midway through the meeting where the federal officials had to try and explain their offer to the media to counter some of the media spin and the rumours that were going around. At that press conference there were three different federal officials literally arguing in front of the media as to whether the $2 billion for the National Children's Agenda was in their own offer or not. By the end of the day there was rampant confusion within our delegation, within their delegation and within the media as to where this $2 billion actually was. I only found out days later that the money was included in the CHST offer, which of course was a negative from our perspective.

You get a sense at a premiers' meeting that if a premier is cutting a deal, he or she has a pretty good idea that the deal has support at home. Usually officials from relevant ministries and the premier's office are on the phone, just checking to make sure that the premier is working within the negotiating parameters that were expected of them back in their home province. However, there are a number of ways you could make the criticism that these meetings are undemocratic. For example, there is often frustration from larger provinces, which are saying, "I get the same vote at such-and-such a meeting as the representatives from a new territory like Nunavut." And in theory they do. Quite often the territories and the smaller provinces will watch the tennis match or chess game between the larger provinces and the federal government at the table and pick a side at the end. They usually will work with whatever consensus has been agreed to. But for the most part you have the chief executives (the premiers) of these governments at the first ministers' level, and ministers at a lower level who are in a very good position to make a deal. If they really wanted to they could cut a federal-provincial deal and then walk away from it and have no accountability. A classic example, historically, of this is the Meech Lake Accord scenario, where two provinces had not really sewed up the support of their legislatures from the back end. And we saw the results of moving too far away from the position that your legislature or your caucus can support.

The first ministers' meeting is a little unusual in that the federal government has a big home court advantage. It's in the Lester B. Pearson building (in Ottawa), and the provinces are told how many staff they can bring. Although the rules are fairly laid out by the federal government with some negotiation with the provinces, it's clear who the boss is. At ministerial meetings you can sometimes get fairly ridiculous groups. I remember in Quebec City, for example, for a meeting of ministers of the environment, Ontario, the largest province, had an unusually large delegation of nine. It was about two or three people larger than normal because we had a replacement minister there who hadn't had time to be briefed on many of these issues. Meanwhile David Anderson, the federal environment minister, who clearly had an agenda at this meeting, brought a delegation of 52, nine of whom had some sort of title putting them in "communications." David Anderson was sitting at the table as a minister of the environment. Behind him there was a huge phalanx of chairs of staff members who spent the meeting sitting there, waiting for the remote chance that the minister might have a question to ask them to help in his negotiating stance. Other provinces bring two or three staff members. Ontario usually brings five or six, and we're the biggest provincial government. Quite often the federal government treats these meetings as an opportunity to roll out the communications infrastructure, to roll out the staff. You have to wonder what the purpose really is of having 50 people in that room, away from home for a couple of days.

In fact, the media is much more central to the process in first ministers' meetings than I think many of the premiers who are involved in these things would want. In the case of the first ministers' meetings, there may be anywhere from 30 to several hundred journalists, and all they worry about is if there is going to be provincial consensus or not on the deal. So what you have is a situation where the media says, "What are our objectives?" and that will be the basis of judgment for the meeting.

The purpose of my job at the first ministers' meeting, and my job with the Ontario Intergovernmental Affairs Department, was to act as a channel between the ongoing negotiations and the reporters who are back outside. It's really troubling for a reporter. You feel some sympathy for them, in a sense, that they have to at the end of the day file a report on a big meeting. And that report is supposed to be important. But they have virtually no information about what's going on inside. Really, they are in a very dependent situation. It is the classic old meaning of the word "spin." They have nothing else to rely on but what a federal spin-doctor is saying on one side of the room and what I, as provincial media relations staff or spin-doctor, am saying to a reporter on the other side of the room.

To a certain degree the microscope of the media skews the decision-making process because the key element for all governments in these meetings is how the result will appear in the media. Quite often first ministers' meetings or ministerial meetings are discussed over nothing more than a so-called communiqué, which is essentially an elegant form of an advance press release. In the case of the health-care deal that was worked out in September of 2000, the objective of the provinces was to get more health-care dollars into provincial coffers. But in our view, the reason for the meeting was that the prime minister wanted to be in a position to stand up and say that he had brokered this deal to demonstrate that he really did care about health care at the provincial level.

To a citizen looking at the system from the outside, it may seem to be irrational. It doesn't make sense that you would be talking about $23 billion in six hours. I want to make it clear from my personal experience, in all of the intergovernmental meetings I've seen, that it's not the players who are being irrational per se. The politicians there are better and smarter and more capable than many people in the public give them credit for. But when you lock any group of 13 or 14 people in a room to make a decision in six hours about anything, you're going to come up with a strange result. Particularly if they know that outside that room they have to justify how they came to a deal, often without knowing all of the details of the impact of that deal itself. It seems a little crazy. Many people I've talked to who were in that environment and have seen those sorts of meetings come away shaking their head and thinking it's some kind of a political hallucination to go through the experience.

But here's the most important point about the September 2000 first ministers' meeting — this meeting was an example of a first ministers' meeting that we didn't need at all. There was nothing stopping the prime minister from restoring the money he cut from health care in 1995. He could have stood in front of a microphone and done it on his own. The beauty of this situation, from his perspective, was the premiers had asked him for this money, so why not get them all in a big room and trot them all out in front of the cameras a few weeks before the 2000 federal election? And the result is you have a headline that says, "Prime minister brokers health-care deal — nation builder" instead of a headline that says, "Prime minister restores money that was cut by his government from health care several years before." It was a meaningful and interesting meeting for the provinces in that they got what they wanted. But the reason they got what they wanted was because they showed up for a necessary photo opportunity (from the PM's point of view) rather than a necessary meeting with the prime minister.

Is Brian Kelcey's perception true, that the whole reason these meetings occur is for political jockeying before the press, and the potential good "spin" they will get back home? Nothing more, nothing less? Is this the proper way to make decisions on billions of dollars? Well, maybe.

Most people regard the spectacle of 10 provincial premiers bickering and fighting with the federal government as useless political drama. I have begun to look at it in a much more optimistic way. When the premiers complain about the federal government, and the prime minister battles them back, Canadians should not be too concerned. They are watching the wheels of a healthy federal system in motion. In many ways, the louder the political fight the better, as one level of government pushes back against another, defending its turf. This is how our system *should* operate.

However, our current federal system of government actually encourages the two levels of government to increase spending of our money in order to protect their own programs. By acting, or in other words spending, each level of government protects and defends its own relevance to its citizens, and relevance in government is everything. If one level of government has jurisdiction over an area of governing but doesn't spend, tax or regulate in that jurisdiction, the rival government, either federal or provincial, will try to move in. From student loans to building roads to health care, Canadian history more than adequately illustrates this reality.

Canadians often tend to overlook one important fact: constitutionally the federal government has no right to be in areas like health care in the first place. So if you are the federal government but you don't have jurisdiction, what do you do? You either flaunt the carrot of increased funding in front of the provinces or you collude. And what we have seen in recent years is collusion dubbed "co-operation" between the two levels of government. It is a troubling trend, not because these levels of government aren't trying to do good for their citizens, but rather because this so-called co-operation permits both levels of government to remain unaccountable for the tax dollars they spend.

Further comments from Brian Kelcey reveal just how blurry jurisdiction over health care has become.

Brian Kelcey, Former Communications Officer, Government of Ontario

There has been a lot of tension lately between provincial governments and the federal government, and one of the reasons is cost-shared programs. Quite often the federal government will say, "We're going to move into this area of jurisdiction," and they use their spending power to start spending in that area. Although this may interfere with a provincial program, there isn't always a debate over the program between the two levels of government.

I can tell you one interesting story that relates to cost sharing. While I was with the Ontario government in 1999, they made a decision to take ads out against the federal government's involvement in health care. That was a very controversial decision, and I know for a fact that it was something the provincial government thought about a great deal. But the situation was this: we had a cost-shared program with the federal government, and they were not holding up their end of the funding bargain. In this type of disagreement there is no mechanism whatsoever to force the two sides to come to a resolution. This is a major problem with Confederation. When you have no dispute resolution mechanism and the federal government has most of the taxing power and few of the responsibilities of program spending, it's a great deal for them.

Since nothing else was working in terms of trying to persuade the federal government politically that it was time to restore the cuts that they put into health care, we had only one political tool remaining. The Ontario government bought advertising and squeezed the federal government to the bargaining table by convincing voters that those cuts should be restored.

Rita Burak, Former Secretary of the Cabinet, Government of Ontario
The expanding health-care budgets have become a tremendous worry in the provinces. Yet the provinces really didn't get too upset about this until they found themselves being criticized by other levels of government about why they had to ration services and amalgamate hospitals. Suddenly the provinces found themselves being criticized by — wait a minute — the federal government.

The province of Ontario wanted to get the explanation across to the public that one of the reasons they had to take these measures in changing the health-care system was because the transfer payments to the provinces that help fund the expenditure of health care were being cut back by the federal government. And the public really wasn't hearing that part of it. The public was seeing some things happen in the health-care system that they didn't like, and they knew that the province was responsible for money going to the hospital sector, so they focused their anger on the Ontario government. And on top of that the Ontario government was getting scorn heaped on it by another level of government. So they said, "Wait a minute, we better let folks know that part of the problem here was the federal government pulling back." I'll bet the average person in

Ontario assumed that the federal and provincial governments were funding health-care costs in the province equally.

The Ontario government took out ads and explained, "Guess what? The federal government is only funding health care to the tune of about 14¢ on the dollar." I personally think it is important for the general public to be informed about who is paying for what in this.

Brian Kelcey, Former Communications Officer, Government of Ontario

The ads were successful from the provincial government's point of view. We were happy to know that, if necessary, you could use ads to get the federal government to the table again, if it was something you needed to do. Our ministry and our government made all sorts of proposals at the time to try and do things in a more intelligent way through a mediation process, but the federal government said no. So the ads worked for us then. I think it's entirely possible that you will see more of that in the future. There will be a point someday when an ad is going to be the solution.

Why did the ads work? Because the public doesn't really know who is supposed to deliver health care in Canada. Now, I don't blame the public because health-care financing, which is really the issue here, is very complex. The provinces, in theory, are the ones who are supposed to be delivering health care. Yet the federal government is moving into more and more grey areas of delivery. I think it's pretty clear that citizens believe the provinces are better at delivering health care because they're right there on the ground seeing the needs of people. So I think the pure educational value of getting that provincial message out is what got the federal government scared enough to come and meet with the provinces and discuss the needs of funding health care in this country.

Donald Savoie, Author of *Governing from the Centre*

The fundamental problem is that the federal government, in constitutional terms, has no business in the health-care field. It doesn't belong there. It has no proper role. It has been there because it raises taxes for the public purse. The federal government has money to offer the provinces to cost-share medical services. Initially they advised the provinces that they would pay 50 percent of the costs, but it's now down in the range of 15 percent. So the federal government's only role in health care is through taxpayers' money. That's where the confusion stems from. Nobody really knows who is responsible for what.

Accountability in cost-sharing arrangements between governments is not obvious. In an ideal world, accountability is relatively simple. In an ideal world, either the federal or provincial governments would be responsible for a program like health care.

Brian Kelcey, **Former Communications Officer, Government of Ontario**
When the federal government sets up these cost-shared funds, quite often its priority is to get visibility and impact in different provinces. This is a real problem. For instance, at the September 2000 meeting Health Minister Allan Rock presented a cost-shared program to buy new MRIs (magnetic resonance imagers) for the provinces. But at that meeting you have a province like Saskatchewan that has problems just maintaining its basic hospitals. Their first priority is not more MRIs. They need basic facilities. They need nurses. They need to cover their basic budgets. However, when the federal government says to a province like that, "We're going to provide funding for MRIs," the public expectation is that of course the provincial government is going to accept free MRIs. In the end the province is left holding the bag, paying the operating funds for these MRIs that may not have been what the province actually needed in the first place.

That's a representative example, but there are many provinces who are saying the same thing: "We have different priorities. If you force us into a cost-shared program that does a specific thing, you are essentially putting us under political pressure to take resources away from things that are our priorities and move them over into an area that you think is a national priority. These things are clearly provincial areas of jurisdiction for a reason, and we know best how to deal with them." Quite often I think the cynics among us in intergovernmental affairs look at a lot of federal funding offers as carrots.

Donald Savoie, Author of *Governing from the Centre*

The federal government provides money and the provinces are the implementers of the programs. This makes trying to figure out who's accountable for what very difficult. It's very difficult for a member of Parliament to tell the prime minister that it is ultimately the provinces that should deliver the program, while the only thing that the federal government should do is provide money and some basic guidelines.

The problem is that the provinces tell the public that Ottawa is not providing enough money for health. Meanwhile the federal government tells the public that it is not the provider of health care; it only provides money. So trying to hold somebody to account in health care is like grabbing smoke. It is very complicated.

Rita Burak, Former Secretary of the Cabinet, Government of Ontario

The federal government could say, "All right, we will pull out of health care, and we will change the tax arrangement, whereby we take less money in taxes from you, the provinces. And you're going to deal with health care 100 percent." But if I were the federal government, would I want to do that? Because what is the rationale for our federal government, if it's not to be a part of some of the fundamental issues that make us Canada? And if the federal government is no longer an important player, what is the role of the federal government?

Rita Burak asks a good question, one that most citizens don't even contemplate. Our Constitution says that Canada is a federation, where the authority for a government to act is divided between two levels of government. Each level of government is sovereign within the limits of its jurisdictions. This division of powers is a necessary mechanism of accountability because it tells citizens who is responsible for doing what. But when "co-operation" between the levels of government occurs, from whom can we as citizens demand results to ensure our tax dollars are spent wisely? Everybody? No one? Toward whom can we point the finger of blame and how do we know how much of our money is going where?

I'm not saying that all cost-shared programs are bad, but our Constitution was not framed with these programs in mind. Moreover, can we be sure that tax dollars raised by one level of government and spent by another are subject to proper auditing and proper management? If we want to use cost-sharing programs, we need to include safeguards and new mechanisms of accountability in our Constitution to control the actions of our various governments. Right now, all levels of government combine to centralize power and decision making while excluding their legislatures to a large degree.

An even worse aspect of cost-shared programs is that they blur the lines of responsibility. In order to make cost-shared programs palatable to all levels of government, the terms of the agreements and the conditions of how the money is spent often become vague at best. This vagueness allows the levels of government as much wiggle room as possible in spending the money, but it also skews the decisions that result.

David Crombie,
Former Federal Cabinet Minister and Former Mayor of Toronto

No level of government is willingly going to give up money, power or exposure. What they will do is share them. A cost-shared program is a way to spend more money than you have.

The difficulty with cost-shared programs is you're spending money that is not yours, and it's always easier to spend more and not be accountable for it. Most people in government agree that the old-fashioned cost-shared programs, with 20 percent here and 15 percent there, or a 25/75 split, institutionalize non-responsibility for the product and usually inflate the costs.

If we walked into a grocery store and I said, "Get what you need and I'll look after 75 percent of it," you'd buy more than you could actually afford. And if you have a program where the other governments are paying 75 percent and you're only paying 25 percent, you'll also spend more; not because you're irresponsible or greedy, but because you have real needs. So they're happy to get these programs. My problem with cost-shared programs has to do with questions of accountability and extending costs.

Brian Kelcey, **Former Communications Officer, Government of Ontario**

Cost-shared programs between the federal and the provincial governments can involve billions of dollars, and a provincial government can be left scrambling to figure out how they're going to implement the dollars that are being offered up to them. Federal governments have often created cost-shared programs where they have said, "We'll come in, we'll pay half the costs for these new services or this new capital spending." The province is more or less obliged to come in and pay as well, otherwise they are declining free money from the federal government. So the provincial minister will sign the deal. The cupcakes are rolled out and the announcement takes place with the federal minister there cutting the ribbons. And a couple years down the road the federal money trickles away and goes toward a new cost-shared program. This is what creates the cynicism between the two levels of government.

Deborah Grey, Reform and Canadian Alliance MP, 1989–Present

The federal government has centralized almost every power they can get their paws on. We have consistently said that we should give the provinces back their original jurisdictional powers over sports, language, culture, housing, municipal affairs, labour-market training and economic development. The problem is they want to keep all that to themselves and look really powerful.

There would be nothing to stop the federal government from saying, "We're going to give those powers back to all the provinces." Not just one, but all of them, and let them look after and administer their own provincial program, which they had been doing for many, many years in the first place. But once you get it you don't want to relinquish it. I get criticized by people who say, "Oh, you just think everything should be ripped apart in Ottawa and have it totally decentralized." You can't do that in a country this size. You need a strong federal government to look after monetary policy, fiscal policy, policing, agriculture and the money market. All those things are very important to keep in Ottawa, but you don't need someone to hang on to every little piece of power.

David Crombie, Former Federal Cabinet Minister and Former Mayor of Toronto

Even as a written guarantee in the Canadian Constitution, the division of powers among levels of government has always been blurry. It still is today. For the first 30 years of Confederation, the federal and provincial governments fought over who did what; even over who could charge tax on booze.

The division of powers among governments in Canada will never be fixed for all time because life changes. People change. Needs change. When a society is doing very well it has different needs than when it isn't doing well. So "who does what" will change. When the war came along in the 1940s, everything changed. In peacetime, good times and bad times, you have to respect those changes.

Cost-shared programs are most effective in cases where there's a clear commitment by a level of government to perform a specific task over a particular duration. Five or 10 years is a commitment.

Brian Kelcey, **Former Communications Officer, Government of Ontario**
There are now a lot of provincial finance ministers telling the public and telling each other in ministers' meetings that they were beginning to see cost-shared programs as liabilities rather than assets. They don't know if the federal government will be carrying its share two or three years down the road when it actually matters.

Richard Marceau, **Bloc Québécois MP, 1997–Present**
I think it's despicable to attach strings to the money from Ottawa. There have been intrusions in education, training, environment, the family and parental leave issues. For example, the Quebec government has come up with a proposal that is going to build a very strong parental leave program that would be much broader than the one the federal government suppos-edly would like to put into place. A lot of people of my genera-tion are self-employed, and according to the federal government's program those people wouldn't be covered by parental leave because the unemployment insurance program is not available to them. We know that self-employed people are usually young and that young people tend to be the ones who have kids, so as a result a big chunk of the younger generation in Canada won't be able to have access to a good parental leave

program. If it was the Quebec program that was being put into place, those self-employed people would already be covered by a parental leave program.

We're saying to Ottawa that if the rest of Canadians are satisfied with the type of programs that the federal government is proposing, fine. In Quebec, however, we set ourselves objectives that are much broader than the ones that are being put into place by Ottawa, so we'd like them to just send us the money and we'll administer it. We'll be better for young Quebecers who want to have children.

The irony is that we have federalists who defend the division of powers between the provincial level and the federal level, saying that they don't care about our provincial jurisdiction and that they are going to invade it. On the other hand, it is the sovereigntists who say that as long as Quebec is in Canada, we'd like to respect the document (the Constitution) upon which the relationship is based. In this situation, therefore, we have sovereigntists defending the letter and the spirit of the Canadian Constitution, which is weird and surreal.

David Crombie,
Former Federal Cabinet Minister and Former Mayor of Toronto

Everybody becomes cynical with funding from different levels of government because they can never be sure what the government is going to do. The federal or provincial government will say, "We're thinking about an infrastructure program." You have no idea what they're thinking or how much money that involves. They don't tell you. It's a lot of game playing, and it need not be so.

To a certain degree one could say that local politicians are just blaming another government for their own problems. It's always easier to blame somebody else, and politicians certainly do that. The federal government blames the provinces. The provinces blame the federal government. That will go on.

Ruth Grier, Former Ontario Cabinet Minister and New Democratic MPP

There's no question in my mind that the existence of a subsidy from a level of government that would not normally be subsidizing a project, regardless of what that project is, skews the decision making because you have an opportunity to save your own money and use somebody else's money to build something that you think ought to be built. And so you move ahead with what you can.

Brian Kelcey, Former Communications Officer, Government of Ontario
These cost-shared programs skew decisions in many cases. Cost-shared programs can be productive. But if they are not carefully designed to fill a specific need, they can be dangerous. They can lead provincial governments to spend money on areas that are not a priority in their particular region or province simply because the money is on the table.

One of the premiers came out of the September 2000 first ministers' meeting saying, "Look, it's hard for a politician to say no when there is money on the table." That is the problem with the cost-shared program when the federal government makes an offer. If you say no to a cost-shared environmental program, absurd as the program may be, it looks to the public, or at least to the media who's reporting it, as though you are refusing the environment. The clear implication — and the federal government feeds this implication — is that you're saying no to the environment in general instead of saying no to working on this set of priorities on the environment. Somehow you're some kind of fool for not taking the federal government's money.

Saying no to "free money" may be political suicide for the provinces, as Brain Kelcey points out, but refusing these dangled financial carrots should perhaps be more popular in the future. As we have seen, decisions about how to spend the money end up distorted, the wrong levels of government end up taxing the wrong citizens for programs and services, and no one does a proper job of overseeing how the money is spent.

How do you get citizens to care about such arcane matters? First, you tell them that the blurry jurisdictional lines between the levels of governments are costing them money — big money. How much? From what I have been able to uncover, nobody knows and nobody keeps track of such information.

Brian Kelcey, Former Communications Officer, Government of Ontario

If there is an area of government in Canada where there isn't overlap, it is a rare thing to find. Increasingly governments in Canada, and certainly our government in Ontario, are finding that they need staff whose job it is solely to be an "intergovernmental staffer." I worked in a ministry called Intergovernmental Affairs for a couple of years, and what we did was identify areas of overlap between the federal government and the provincial government.

Virtually in every ministry there are different kinds of overlap. There is minor overlap in terms of provision of Aboriginal services. There is increasing overlap in health care, transport and infrastructure. There is overlap in terms of the environmental issues. These are a big source of tension because provincial and federal governments have different policies and priorities in these areas. There are departments and units in the Ontario government like the Intergovernmental Finance Unit, which is in the Ministry of Finance, just to figure out how all the money is being transferred back and forth between the governments.

It becomes a considerable drain on people's resources just to understand what intergovernmental relationships they are committed to, as opposed to focusing on the delivery of programs.

David Crombie,
Former Federal Cabinet Minister and Former Mayor of Toronto

Generally speaking, most people are uncertain about which level of government delivers the services that they receive. There are some organized groups of civic society in municipalities, such as business associations and ratepayers' groups, which do know. The people who do know what level of government delivers a program are a small number of insiders within the system.

Most people don't know what the federal government does. They know that the local government looks after the roads and the sidewalks, but they don't really know with any great precision. Secondly, they don't really care. They know that it should be done more efficiently and democratically, but beyond that, politicians and bureaucrats care more about how government works than voters and citizens do.

People should have some reasonable intelligence about how government works; that's part of being a citizen. But they shouldn't be expected to follow the vicissitudes of how much money is spent by this government on this part of a service because it's all very complicated; much more complicated than it was 100 years ago.

Brian Kelcey, Former Communications Officer, Government of Ontario
To a certain degree, all of this overlap is very frustrating for people working in a level of government, as I did in Intergovernmental Affairs, but it's much more frustrating to the citizen. As a citizen, if you're looking to find out who to complain to that your hospital isn't working, for example, or you are worried that there isn't enough funding of roads for the expanding City of Ottawa, or if you are complaining that there are problems with your environment because you're a resident living on the Great Lakes, you don't know who to pick up the phone and complain to. In some ways it provides advantages to those governments because it allows them in desperate situations to finger point at one another and say, "It's not my fault."

It has certainly been the official view of the Ontario government that we could use some clarity in how things are run in this country, when it comes to accountability for dollars. And while I'm sure the federal government will point back and say, "Ontario has invaded our jurisdiction now and again," I think more and more governments, like the Ontario government, are standing up and saying, "Let's try and get some clarity. Let's work out who does what."

So until our system of government in its entirety learns to say no — and mean no — areas of jurisdiction will not be clear. Until the lines of control and communication are clear you will always have the temptation for one government or another to step in and say, "We can get more political mileage out of solving this problem more quickly than the next level of government." I think this is the source for a great deal of the government overlap that has been created.

I don't believe that the provincial governments are to blame for the problems that we have with clarity. But I think, genuinely and objectively, as a citizen as well as a political staffer, that the provinces are the much more honest partners. I have seen the federal government step into areas where it makes no sense, time and time again. But in the end, wouldn't we all like a country where we can at least figure out whose fault it is?

Indeed it would be nice if we could instill some accountability back in our system of government. We should have the proper level of government delivering the right services, and our Constitution does a good job of delineating these responsibilities. Perhaps we should all read it one of these days.

Clarity is important in politics. "Who does what" is important in politics. Without clarity and boundaries of responsibility, citizens do not know where to turn or where to demand answers. If citizens can understand who does what, their demands on the system as consumers of government programs and services would be more efficiently met and mistakes would be corrected more quickly. Our costs, in terms of tax dollars, might even fall. Each level of government could focus on its proper areas of jurisdiction instead of trying to be all things to all people. But politicians have an interest in keeping the waters murky: this makes it easier for them to shift the blame and take the credit whenever the opportunity arises.

CHAPTER 5

The Media and Question Period:

A New Theatre of the Absurd

What impact does the media have on Parliament and what role do MPs play with regard to the media?

First ministers' meetings have become, for all intents and purposes, a media show where deals are supposedly brokered. The media bestows verdicts of success or failure upon these intergovernmental meetings, even if little or nothing has been accomplished. The agenda of these meetings is set months before they take place, based on a set of premises that the first ministers prearrange. Nonetheless, it is interesting to watch the news about these first ministers' meetings during the week leading up to them. You can see the political jostling as the various premiers set our their "demands" on the prime minister. For his part, the prime minister knows exactly what he wants to showcase to the public, to whom he repeatedly expresses the hope that he and the provinces "can make progress." At every first ministers' meeting these little charades occur for the benefit of the media, and like good soldiers they fall in line and stake out the various sides in the federal-provincial battle for their audiences.

During the meetings the premiers and the prime minister are always aware that there are about 200 hungry reporters waiting on their every utterance. Conflict always makes for a better story than co-operation, so the various spin-doctors at both levels of government feed the ravenous journalists everything they can to get their message out.

But what about Parliament and the influence the media have had in Ottawa?

Of all the subjects covered in this book, this one offers the most non-partisan glimpse at what has happened to Parliament. People from all sides of the political spectrum believe that the changes that have occurred in media over the past 30 years, especially in television, have hurt the institution of Parliament. They see that politicians live and die by the media and that this has detracted from the job of overseeing the government. The microscopic scrutiny of the media has forced politicians to play the game of trying to get as much media exposure as they can. Visibility, recognition, TV airplay and acceptance by the Ottawa media elite are what many politicians today believe they need to get ahead. They are probably right. The media vastly impacts the view citizens have of the political stage today.

Nearly every person we talked to about Parliament managed to turn their answers around to insert their views on the Canadian media. Many MPs feel that preoccupation with image, sensationalism and an appetite for controversy in reporting have taken a front seat over serious, issue-driven journalism. Others, like former industry minister Brian Tobin, feel the media has played an important role in making government more transparent and accountable. So who is right?

Brian Tobin, Former Liberal MP and Cabinet Minister

We've never had such a broadly based capacity to know what's happening to us as citizens, or to participate in the political process if we choose to, and to find ways to make ourselves heard. We live in a time when the average citizen has access to information in more ways and at greater speed and accuracy than ever before. We have news organizations, newspapers, radio and Internet access, which is instantaneous and can provide complete coverage of what's happening all across this country. We have two news networks that operate 24 hours a day and more newspapers and reporters on Parliament Hill than ever before. We also have the Access to Information Act, which allows citizens to inspect the details of government correspondence and records. None of those instruments existed 50, 60 or 70 years ago. Parliamentarians came to Ottawa by train once or twice a year and then they went back. Other than that, they operated here behind closed doors.

None of this is to suggest in any way, shape or form that we shouldn't be tough-minded in holding governments accountable. Not at all. Governments should be challenged by the media and by the opposition and certainly can be more open and more transparent. The system has become and continues to become far more open and responsive to what's happening, primarily because of technology. It is amazing how our democracy of today is far more open and transparent than the democracy of yesterday, especially in the way the voices of people who live all across Canada are reflected right back to the policy makers.

Donald Savoie, Author of *Governing from the Centre*

I think the major change we've seen in terms of MPs' emphasis in Parliament has been driven by the media. If you want to understand the role of a member of Parliament, look at the media because the member of Parliament will play to what the media wants. We have the 15-second clip on TV and that's what a member of Parliament seeks. You can't understand a government policy or a government program in a 15-second clip.

Reg Alcock, Liberal MP, 1993–Present

There once was much greater individual authority in the House of Commons and in the way committees functioned. Television changed that. Television, when it first came on the scene, was a hot medium. It needed an image, and focused on leaders right across the industrialized world. This concentration of power, over a period of 30 or 40 years, slowly moved to the centre. When you step outside of the 30-second TV sound bite, you step into a world of great complexity. Television is a medium that likes simple stories. So it was easier to focus on a leader than it was to focus on a whole group of people.

Patrick Boyer, Progressive Conservative MP, 1984–1993

The speeches that are given by rank-and-file members of Parliament are not getting on the national news. It's only what is said by the prime minister, the Cabinet minister or a leader of the opposition that gets attention because the media themselves have decided to just focus on the very apex of power, which is a self-defeating circle over time in terms of a representative democracy.

Bill Blaikie, New Democratic MP, 1979–Present

When I got to Parliament in 1979 there was considerably more scrutiny in terms of the committee having an opportunity to question the Cabinet ministers. The ministers spent more time there than they do now and committees were covered more. So you always had a Canadian Press guy sitting in committee. I think in some ways TV coverage has been hard on that kind of scrutiny because real scrutiny doesn't lend itself to a 30-second clip, whereas reporting a prolonged dialogue between a member and a Cabinet minister is more suitable for print media. And there was more of that 20 years ago than there is today.

Donald Savoie, Author of *Governing from the Centre*

The media has changed as well — it is now 24-hour news. It's a more aggressive and less deferential media. So a member of Parliament will try to sniff out what it is that the media wants or what the flavour of the month is. That tends to defocus a lot of members of Parliament and I think that's a fundamental change. But to really get at a government program and for an MP to hold a government to account, you have to do a lot of homework. The question is, will a member of Parliament be willing to invest that kind of effort to hold a government to account on a given program? In most cases the answer is no.

The short-term nature of "all media, all the time" has driven an urgency into Parliament. Whether you are on the government side or in the opposition, the feeling is, get your message out quick and hurt your opponent.

This focus on the short term, and on trying to score the 15-second sound bite on the evening news, has created an atmosphere that many politicians describe as the "dumbing down" of Parliament.

Keith Martin, Reform and Canadian Alliance MP, 1993–Present

We as Opposition should be dealing with important issues, but when we try to do so, people in the media say, "Oh, that's boring." The media want to deal with the sensational rather than the substantive, and we fall in with that. In my view we should be dealing with the substantive issues more and the sensational ones less, in the hope that the media will catch up to us. At least we should keep trying. But at the end of the day, if we don't put our message out to the public and the media is the interface upon which we work, we are dead in the water. So we have to find a balance. I hope that in the future the public will demand that the media portray what is happening in Parliament more accurately, that the public will get more involved and that the Opposition will focus on more of the big issues.

Dennis Mills, Liberal MP, 1988–Present

I think that the media are primarily responsible for Parliament becoming a dumbed-down organization. I call this hall right outside the House of Commons "hooker alley." It's where dozens and dozens of journalists hang out after Question Period and look for quotes and clips from members and ministers.

There are a lot of journalists on the Hill who take the time to write in-depth, substantive pieces. But a number of journalists just hang around in hooker alley day in and day out, looking for the 15- or 30-second TV clip. And I don't think that it represents the essence of what's happening here.

Michael Harris, Journalist and Author

I think one of the poverties in journalism today is that the sort of stuff I like to do, which is to take a subject to book length, is hardly ever done. Most news agencies can't afford it, and it's questionable whether it would hold the public's attention. There is the 15-second clip that everyone reads, but there's no follow-up story the next day. It's partially lazy journalism, but it's also easy journalism. It's like coming out and having your lunch from a buffet that someone lays out every day.

A recent example is the whole thing about there being "no prices" in medicare. I did an in-depth interview with Minister of Health Allan Rock for two hours about whether or not that was true, and if it wasn't true, what had to be done to have things fixed. He gave very substantive answers, but I think the story only made page nine in my newspaper. In another newspaper we were on the front page one day, but the next day's latest rage had nothing to do with medicare. The norm has become this daily buffet of going from one subject to the next and covering mostly personality-driven stories. So yes, it's easy, it's lazy, and it's also the kind of *People* magazine ethic that's come to television.

I'm not sure who started the process, but I think the end result — that the news has been dumbed down — is irrefutable. As a person who's essentially a writer, I would think that we have a chance to change that, just as the MP has a chance to change their now impotent role in our parliamentary system. It comes down to individual journalists working hard and selling stories to editors, but so far I haven't seen a lot of examples of that. You can count on the fingers of one hand the number of investigative reporters whose work has made a real difference in this country. Andrew McIntosh has done some fine work. Jim Bronskill of the *Ottawa Citizen* is another example. But they are not the norm of the hundreds of journalists who work Parliament Hill; these two people are the exception, and surely to goodness one would think that there's a little more room for some others.

It's a harsh judgment of some of my colleagues, and they probably wouldn't make me president of the Press Club tomorrow, but I wasn't in danger of being that anyway. I think that the business of journalism is about the reader, the viewer or the listener. I don't think it's about the people who purvey the news, who come in every day and purport to cover the news. It's about who's looking at it, the end user. I'm more concerned about their judgment — expressed in the number of books sold, number of letters to the editor or the number of mistakes they point out — rather than how many kudos you get from your buddies.

Television, I must say, is the hammer that most people use to pin down the news these days, not reading. You know, if you ask yourself, "Who is the most powerful journalist in the country?" I think you'd be hard-pressed to come up with an easy answer. It used to be people like Jeff Simpson — the commentary people, people of substance who knew the system, knew Ottawa, and had a cultural memory. Now it's basically a dogfight every day to see who gets the best clip. I don't think any journalist individually is powerful, it's the medium of television, one medium out of the many that we have covering Parliament, which is the most powerful.

Harry Swain, Deputy Minister of Industry, 1992–1995
We used to refer to *The Globe and Mail* as a test. If you were concerned about how to play some action, you asked yourself, how would this look if it were reported in *The Globe and Mail* tomorrow morning? Unless you had a happy answer to that, you'd better not do it. The government is like any other organization: what entity likes to admit its mistakes, particularly if they're going to be on the front page of the paper tomorrow morning?

For better or for worse, the media wields substantial power and influence. The media affects the way issues are handled, even to the point of determining their outcome. As history has shown, the media can bring a political career into the limelight — look at John Manley after the terrorism of September 11, 2001 — or the media can end a career — look at Cabinet minister Hedy Fry. Fry made numerous errors as a minister, but the nail in her coffin occurred when the media caught her speaking to Parliament claiming that racists were burning crosses in Prince George "as I speak." Although the prime minister supported her for a short while, it was clear Fry had lost her credibility with the media, who along with the opposition parties ensured the story had a long public life. She eventually became an embarrassment to the government. With her career in tatters, she was dumped from Cabinet in the January 2002 shuffle.

Foreign media coverage of political events in Canada can also force the Canadian government into action on various fronts. For example, the subsidization of the Canadian film industry (including the massive labour tax credits our film crews receive) has been widely and negatively reported on throughout the U.S. Even Hollywood's top lobbyist, Jack Valenti, has asked the U.S. government to take political action against Canada at the World Trade Organization for, in his view, unfairly subsidizing Canadian workers and killing jobs in Hollywood. The media coverage (and resulting political pressure) have forced the Canadian government to publicly address this issue both in Los Angeles and at home, with foreign "goodwill" tours and an almost daily defence of "Canadian culture."

In Canada political dramas often live or die by the media coverage they receive. The Human Resources Development Canada (HRDC) "Billion-Dollar Boondoggle," as the media headlines dubbed it in 2000, was a story that lasted about four weeks. Despite the fact that over $1 billion was spent on various job-creation schemes, with little or no accounting of where the money went or if the money served its purpose, the media (and the public) gradually tired of the story. The government rode out the political storm, stood by HRDC Minister Jane Stewart, and eventually the public forgot about the issue. Interestingly, the program, now renamed, still receives approximately the same federal budget appropriation that it did prior to the story breaking.

Another interesting political drama that lived and died by the media was the Oka crisis of 1990.

Harry Swain, Deputy Minister of Industry, 1992–1995

I had a lot of experience with the media. For example, during the Oka summer (the standoff between the Canadian military and a small group of Mohawk at the Oka Native reserve lasted the entire summer of 1990), I was the deputy minister of Indian affairs. That was a pretty interesting national issue. The media reported what I had to say about it early on in the summer, and in a way that made me uncomfortable. Later in the summer it became clear to us on the government side that the way in which the media was reporting the story — and not what we were doing — was having more effect on how the Mohawks were responding to us and the public. The whole affair at Oka continued until the time that the people there no longer had easy access to the media. Once we realized that we could cut off their cellphone use, and with it their access to the media, the effort collapsed fairly quickly.

Donald Savoie, Author of *Governing from the Centre*

The Wall Street Journal, if you recall, ran a piece during the budget process in 1995 saying that Canada was close to hitting the wall in terms of public spending. Mexico had hit the wall and *The Wall Street Journal* said Canada, the neighbour to the north, was next in line. That sent a bolt of lightning into Ottawa. The prime minister and the minister of finance were trying to curtail and cut spending. That article was a tremendous help. It gave them the levers to make sure what they wanted done was done. They were able to cut spending programs, review 50,000 jobs and cut many of them. That was a critical moment. It was an external force that came from New York but it was a powerful force that influenced and shaped the kind of decision making that takes place in Ottawa.

Stanley Hartt, Former Chief of Staff to Prime Minister Brian Mulroney

There was a communications department in the Prime Minister's Office that tried to plan how we could present our initiatives in the best possible way. That's only normal, and every prime minister has always done that whether he had a formal apparatus to do it or not. Every press release, every ministerial announcement, every photo opportunity was designed to get people to understand why the government thinks that it's doing the right thing.

I don't think that's media management. It's getting your message out in a way that the public might be receptive to. That people might actually get to understand why you're doing all these strange things, like we did with the GST. Even today you've got to explain to people why we have that excellent, excellent policy. Most people accept it, but the people who really understand — economists and businesspeople — love it as policy. Most ordinary people are resigned to it, but they would still like to see it removed. I think they'd be wrong. So obviously we didn't "manage the media" on that issue.

Gord Lovelace, Former Senate Communications Director

Ottawa is a town based on image. This is a company town, as you might have noticed, a factory where politics is used to manufacture legislation and laws. So certainly image plays a role, otherwise you don't get to be a player because nobody votes for you. For example, the way to get rid of somebody in this town is not to criticize them, slam them or hammer them. The real way to get rid of somebody is to embarrass him or her. To give you a case in point, in 1998 then–solicitor general Andy Scott had a little personal conversation on the plane saying some things he politically shouldn't have, discussing the potential outcome of the APEC inquiry. That was overheard by an opposition MP (Dick Proctor, NDP). It wasn't the resultant hammering of the opposition that really got to him. As a matter of fact, he denied he said anything wrong on the plane, and everybody on the government side said he should stay on as solicitor general. But once the routine started getting on radio and TV and in the newspapers, actually making fun of him, he became an embarrassment for the government. As soon as he became an embarrassment and indeed got embarrassed — and it's pretty hard to embarrass a politician — then he disappeared.

Managing the media may be seen as an attempt to control public opinion, or at least as an attempt to control its influence. While the Prime Minister's Office registers the media as one of their concerns, they do claim not to have a media management agenda as such. This assertion is questionable.

All the research that went into the writing of this book suggests that the Prime Minister's Office and almost every ministry and department of the federal government play a media game that has immense influence on public perception. The ways in which the government's own programs are perceived by the public and the media message that is attached to every government initiative are of paramount importance. The government's own phone book lists literally dozens of communications staff in every department whose job it is to manage the government's message, not to mention the throngs of political attachés that populate every minister's office.

One stark example of this government media monolith came across my desk quite coincidentally during 1999, when we were working on a documentary about the Canada Infrastructure Works Program

(CIWP). We wanted to see if the $8.3 billion spent on that program did what the government said it would do: create jobs and restore Canada's crumbling infrastructure.

When we registered Access to Information requests for information available to the minister on the success of the program, one of the files that came back was a 1,000-page review. Wow, I thought, this will be great. I thought I would get an overview of how the money was spent. I only wish that were the case.

It was chock-full of critiques on whether the program did what it was supposed to do *politically*. In a nutshell, the report was meant to monitor the media and, by extension, the public's reaction to the Canada Infrastructure Works Program. Questions were posed throughout asking whether the media had bought into the job-creation spin the government put on the program. The report also asked if the public *believed* the program was putting people back to work — if they were getting "the message" the government had intended.

The review of the Canada Infrastructure Works Program may be only one case, but if we extend its implications to how the government as a whole operates, we are presented with a discomfiting picture of questionable priorities and motivations. The bottom line is that the media are far more influential than those at the top of the government want us to believe.

I also discovered something interesting about the media delirium that follows Question Period every day, just after 3:00 p.m. in the foyer of the House of Commons. Seeking to witness our MPs interact directly with the media, I inserted myself into the middle of these "media scrums" for several weeks.

Because they see the media interviewing people on TV on the nightly news, viewers are inclined to think that their MPs talk to media for a long time. But these encounters last only 10 or 15 minutes. The reporters run from one MP or Cabinet minister to another, and although they may not even know who is being "scrummed" next to them, they jump on the back of the pack and prod with their microphones for a potential news hit. When it's over, just minutes after the media frenzy began, you could hear a pin drop in the empty foyer.

The media horde that MPs flocked to after Question Period made one wonder at how the current, seemingly nonsensical interaction between the media and parliamentarians came to be. It turns out the answer has more to do with a systemic ailment that has stricken the House of Commons. An ailment that in turn has transformed Question Period into little more than a scripted media spectacle.

Peter Dobell, Director, The Parliamentary Centre

Fifty years ago Question Period lasted about 10 minutes a week. Ministers were questioned on some subject about which there had been late-breaking news and the opposition reasonably considered that they should find out a bit more. The questions were what you might call open, honest. And the answers were open and honest. The system began to change in 1956 when Diefenbaker used Question Period as an instrument for attacking the government on the Mackenzie pipeline debate. He used that day after day, and quite effectively. It changed more when the Liberals were decimated in 1958. There were what were known as the Four Horsemen — Lester Pearson, Paul Martin, Sr., Lionel Chevrier and Jack Pickersgill. They used Question Period so aggressively on Diefenbaker's government that sometimes it lasted all day. It was at that stage that MPs negotiated and agreed to limit it to one hour a day.

George Baker, Liberal MP, 1974–2002

The greatest power of sanctions in the House of Commons lies with the leader of the official Opposition because that's the prize position for asking questions. The Opposition monopolizes Question Period. They can embarrass the government. In other countries' parliamentary systems you can't do this because you have to give 48 hours' notice of your questions.

For an ordinary government backbencher in Canada, Question Period is where the action takes place. But the party whip determines who gets to ask questions. The Speaker is given a list to follow. Where does that leave the government backbenchers? They can't ask any questions. Under other systems there is no such list, no such control. In other systems an ordinary member of Parliament, a backbencher, has more power than a Canadian MP has.

Deborah Grey, Reform and Canadian Alliance MP, 1989–Present

In many respects the leader of the Opposition has a powerful position in Canada because all eyes are on him or her to hold the government accountable. But you don't have the levers of power to actually effect change because you don't have enough arms to go up at voting time. Until you're there in government, and you can write the legislation and win the votes in the House of Commons, it's still the Prime Minister's Office that's in charge.

Brian Tobin, Former Liberal MP and Cabinet Minister

Ours is the most accountable democracy in the world by virtue of the test of daily Question Period, which is pretty thorough, particularly if there's an urgent or emerging issue that we have to respond to. In the British parliamentary system the prime minister and ministers are given notice of the day they're going to have to ask questions and they're given in advance the questions that they have to answer. In our system we go to the House of Commons and we have no idea what questions are going to be asked, but are expected to answer them on the spot as best we can. It's a very transparent and accountable system. Beyond all of this, of course, there are many opportunities to talk to members of the press, who will ask questions and demand answers.

Peter Dobell, Director, The Parliamentary Centre

I don't admire the current Question Period. But it does one thing: it forces the minister to inform himself, or be informed by his advisors, about problems in his department or her department. And if it's a serious problem, to try and rectify it or at least to correct it. Question Period does give the opposition a focus of attack. Unfortunately the media now really only follow Question Period. It gives the television media, particularly, something that they can use.

George Baker, Liberal MP, 1974–2002

The argument could be made that the government is not held accountable for substantive things because under our system Question Period is the only opportunity to deal with them.

The opposition parties and their leaders should be held accountable for what they aren't pursuing in the *only* forum that they have to make the government accountable — Question Period.

Our Question Period becomes a political game of trying to embarrass the government. The questions are limited to 25 seconds, with 34 seconds for an answer. It's the short term all over again. It's not the long term.

Dennis Mills, Liberal MP, 1988–Present

The reality is that, as 99 percent of members of Parliament would tell you, Question Period is orchestrated. It's not a genuine event. The questions are anticipated. They're generated from the morning newspapers or clips on morning television, so the real dynamic of MPs on either side of the House responding spontaneously to things doesn't happen.

John Crosbie,
Progressive Conservative MP, 1984–1993, and Former Cabinet Minister

The House of Commons today is a TV adjunct. The only thing that counts is Question Period. The opposition parties spend all morning thinking up questions to embarrass the government. And the government spends all morning thinking up answers to possible questions and wondering how they can put down the other guy. This show goes on every afternoon in Question Period, and that's all that Parliament amounts to anymore.

The fact that the House of Commons has become nothing more than a "TV adjunct" should be a warning to all Canadians that something is wrong with how we govern ourselves. Do we want a scripted short-term shouting match in the House of Commons to be the citizens' only forum in which to discuss deep issues facing the nation? If Parliament for all intents and purposes now amounts solely to a cantankerous Question Period "media event," why have it at all?

No matter how one observes the current state of affairs, the underlying symptom remains — Question Period has consumed the daily lives of the majority of our MPs. They have become institutionally compelled and coerced to follow its rules. The amount of time spent preparing for Question Period on both sides of the political fence is staggering.

Stanley Hartt, Former Chief of Staff to Prime Minister Brian Mulroney

Public opinion affects the Prime Minister's Office instantaneously. Our routine used to be that we would meet at 7:00 in the morning, the entire staff having read a précis of every newspaper in Canada, basically. We had a clipping service that worked for us all night, and these very thick books were delivered to our homes before 6:00 a.m. We showed up at the office by 7:00, having read them. So we knew what was on the mind of the press all across Canada. That was helpful to prepare for Question Period. Invariably Question Period is based on matters that are already running in the press in order for the opposition member asking the question to have some legs to his question. At least some reporters will be interested in the questions he's asking as well as the answers, and they'll write another article the next day. Knowing what was on the mind of the press also helped us to manage where public opinion was. We were very, very, very interested in public opinion and in keeping ourselves abreast of it.

Unfortunately the relationship with the press makes the PMO job hectic. You have to have smooth, no-error baseball. You can't say, "Look, we'll play an ordinary nine-inning game, or we'll take six or seven errors, as long as we get 12 hits, a couple of which are home runs, that's a good game." We have to play error-free baseball. What makes it hectic is the pressure from the press to create a rabbit that's a distraction from what the prime minister wants to achieve, namely getting his agenda in the public's mind and then through Parliament and into legislation.

Deborah Grey, Reform and Canadian Alliance MP, 1989–Present

In Ottawa I get up at 6:00 and am in the office by 7:00. We have strategy meetings, preparing for Question Period, at 8:00 in the morning. My staff is all in by the time I get back from that meeting, around quarter to nine. Then I do media interviews, have a committee sitting and then get ready for Question Period.

The leader of the Opposition does not sit in our morning meetings and determine who's going to ask each question. We have a strategy team involved in that. It's my job in Question Period to get the prime minister off his scripted notes. That's the job I have. That's the part I love about it, living on the edge.

When the prime minister gets pretty freewheeling, it's emotion, rather than the facts and figures. He goes off into these long explanations about how wonderful he is and how he's been around since 1963. If he's not reading, "Why I love my country," you never know what he's going to say. It's important for me to find out what the prime minister might just kind of go off on a tangent about because that's when Canadians get a chance to see him freewheeling, and lots of times they don't like what they see. I think Canadians deserve a chance to see that.

Question Period is an avenue to be able to kind of draw some of those attitudes out from the prime minister and government members. I'd like to think that I could ask a question in Question Period and get an answer. But I've been there for almost 12 years and I've rarely seen that happen, which is a pity.

Ted McWhinney, Liberal MP, 1993–2000

When I was a parliamentary secretary, one of the roles was substituting for the minister in Question Period, so the briefings for me would begin with the ministry, even in areas that I was well acquainted with. They'd come at 11:00 a.m. and I would already have read the government books. We'd begin discussing potential questions and answers, and we would go right on until 1:30 p.m., and then you would go in the Cabinet room and rehearse the sort of answers to give to questions and make sure your answers co-ordinated with government policy. I would see the Bloc Québécois people begin work at 8:00 in the morning on the Question Period. So between 8:00 a.m. and 3:00 p.m. their time is taken up with this. Is it an efficient use of time, when other problems in Parliament should be addressed?

Television has accentuated this trend, and Parliament has been transformed even more.

Bill Blaikie, New Democratic MP, 1979–Present

Because of the way the media uses the television clips they get from Question Period, they tend to reward the wrong kind of behaviour.

If you've got to reward the wrong behaviour all the time by putting that kind of behaviour on the national news, that's the kind of behaviour you'll get because publicity becomes a substitute for substance or for real accomplishment.

An example of this goes back to 1985. There was a PCB spill around Kenora, Ontario, and I was the NDP environment critic. The spill happened on the weekend, and so we're all back here on Monday, eager to ask questions of the government on this issue. The minister of the environment at the time was Suzanne Blais-Grenier, and on the Monday I asked a couple of questions in Question Period about what the department was doing. I was information-seeking, constructive, not sort of trying to blame her or anything like that. That night on the news, nothing. People started to call my office: "How come the NDP doesn't care about the PCB spill? You guys never raised it ! ... Oh, you did. Well, I never saw it."

So on the Tuesday, a bit more stubborn, I ask a second series of constructive questions. Again, nothing on the news and more calls from citizens: "I thought you guys cared about the environment. This lake's filling up with PCBs and you guys don't care."

On Wednesday morning we sat there, Jim Fulton (NDP MP from Skeena, B.C.) and I, and we said, "All right, we're going to fix this. You go in, you do this. I'll go in, I'll wave my hands around, raise hell, call for the resignation of the minister." So we went in and we scripted it and raised hell in Question Period. That night, I'm all over the news, and everybody's saying, "Great job, Bill."

Now, the problem is, I thought I was doing a better job on the Monday and Tuesday.

CHAPTER 6

Spending Money:
The Madness of Parliament

Although the preceding chapters may depict a troubling view of how the Parliament of Canada operates, this chapter, on how Parliament spends our taxes, is truly distressing.

After every election or in the opening of a new Parliament, the Speech from the Throne, in which the government sets out its plans for the coming session, is read by the governor general to Parliament and to the citizens of the country. During throne speeches there are usually many grand announcements, such as new young offenders law or new foreign policy initiatives. But mainly the Throne Speech is full of the government's intentions to spend money on established or new government programs. Regrettably almost nobody pays attention to the final words of these speeches, or notes how profound they are: "Members of the House of Commons, you will be asked to appropriate funds required to carry out the services and expenditures authorized by Parliament."

That is right. The government cannot spend one red cent without Parliament's authority. In other words, the constitutional duty to oversee all spending on behalf of the citizenry belongs ultimately to Parliament and to the MPs, not to the government of the day. To highlight the importance of this role, I have reprinted the following quote from the Office of the Auditor General's Web site, which reports to Parliament on how wisely the government is spending our money and how efficiently it is delivering our services:

> The people's right to control how public funds are collected and spent is one of the cornerstones of democratic government. In Canada, like other parliamentary democracies, the control is carried out on behalf of the people by their elected representatives, the members of Parliament ... The government of the day must obtain the permission of Parliament before it can collect or spend money. After it spends the public funds, the government must report on its use of the money authorized by Parliament. The obligation of government to answer for its actions is called accountability.[1]

The prose may be dry, but note the importance placed on members of Parliament to hold the government accountable. Members of Parliament are vested with the duty to control the public purse.

They have been entrusted to oversee what is called "supply," which is the traditional word for money. Supply equals money. The Parliament must "supply" the government with the money it needs to act. Without money the government cannot work.

Anne Cools, Liberal Senator, 1984–Present

Parliament really is about two things, just as government is really supposed to be about two things. It is about the authority to raise and spend taxes. In other words, who is given the power, by being voted in, in an election, to dig into the citizens' pockets, to take out money, and who is given the authority to spend it? We used to call that, in Parliament, the "control of the purse." That used to be the most important role of Parliament. And it is our job, as Parliament, to hold governments accountable for every penny that they spend. That's what we're supposed to do.

Marlene Catterall, Liberal MP, 1997–Present; Current Government Whip

The spending priorities of a government indicate where its social, economic, cultural and environmental priorities are. Where the money goes is where the government's going, frankly. I don't think of money as the be all and end all of everything government does, but if you don't get the dollars accounted for, you cannot do the things you want to do.

The fundamental role of Parliament is to decide what resources the government should have, what they're able to spend them on, and to hold the government accountable for meeting what Parliament has approved. If we're not doing that, then we're not exercising full public accountability in the interests of the tax-payers, but also in the interests of Canadian society, which is supposed to benefit from government programs and services.

The important factor is that members of Parliament are not now using the capacity they have to hold government accountable, to have more influence on spending priorities and therefore to have more influence on the policy priorities of government.

Anne Cools, Liberal Senator, 1984–Present

"Control of the purse" is part of the whole phenomenon of supply. That definition of "supply," like so many parliamentary terms, is now somewhat arcane.

Governments have grown increasingly remote and distanced from people. But the fact is that supply means the lifeblood of government. In other words — money. The business of supply is the parliamentary business of voting on money to allow a government to function.

Not voting on supply will bring a government to its knees. If Parliament ever wanted to cripple a government, or to force a government into a state of resignation or defeat, all that the Parliament has to do is cut off supply. It was through this process that the genius of the British constitution excelled and made itself felt. It was through this process of supply, and what we called in Parliament "confidence votes," that despots and absolutists and improper tyrants could be removed without shedding a drop of blood, or without even too much conflict.

It is a fascinating historical process and it was the genius of the parliamentary system. It had a way to excise tyrants and it had a way to excise absolutists, bad rulers, with just a vote of the Parliament of the land. All that the vote had to say was that this chamber has no more confidence in those ministers or in that government.

It's a mighty process, but I fear that this critical role of the parliamentary system is slipping away from us. Its very knowledge seems to be becoming more distant to so many, particularly members of Parliament. The business of mastering this process of controlling money, of even understanding it and being able to guide it — swerve it, correct it and challenge it — is so enormous that it inhibits most MPs, and many shrink back from it.

John Stewart, Liberal MP, 1962–1968; Senator, 1984–1999

The business of supply is fundamental to responsible government. A government could go perhaps years without changing the ordinary laws of the land, or even the tax laws, because they continue from year to year. But the rule of the Constitution is that supply lasts for only one year at a time. That's why the business of supply is so important. Money is the lifeblood of government.

The spending estimates are extremely important because it's through the Estimates — through the control that the House of Commons has on money — that the government is kept responsible to the House of Commons. Unless the Estimates are dealt with properly, that responsibility gets thinner and thinner.

Anne Cools, Liberal Senator, 1984–Present

The government today spends close to $170 billion per year. Amounts of money like this are really beyond the comprehension of most human beings, beyond even their grasp. I sit on the national finance committee because it was my job to bring in the government supply bills. The numbers are staggering — $10 million for this, $10 billion for that, $50 million, $800 million for that. And all of these huge amounts are one-line items.

We have a duty to be stewards of our government institutions, and we have a greater duty to be the protectors and the stewards of our population. For example, when government says they are instituting a gun registry, a member of Parliament should be persuaded to vote or not vote based on the information that is put before them. So if a government tells Parliament that this gun registry will cost $85 million, and then X years later we hear the number is up to $650 million and climbing, then I think it is in order, within the best country in the world, to ask the very best questions. And the best questions are, why did the government tell us that it would cost $85 million, and why is the evidence pointing in an opposite direction?

Spending money is an important function of government. Indeed, it is the most important function. Without money the government cannot govern. To quote an old adage, there are only two sure things in life: death and taxes. The government needs taxes — our money — to fuel itself.

How is Parliament doing today as far as examining and accounting for money? No matter from what side of the political fence they came, among the people my colleagues and I spoke to we couldn't find anyone who stated that Parliament is doing a good job. The bottom line is that Parliament today shows a serious lack of fiscal scrutiny.

Keith Martin, Reform and Canadian Alliance MP, 1993–Present

An example of lack of accountability is the inadequate scrutiny of how Parliament spends money. Even members within government haven't got a clue where the money is going. Money is poured in. The outcomes are not measured. The auditor general alone is doing a very good job of keeping track of where money has gone, but despite the fact that her reports are very eloquent, the important suggestions are always ignored. Why? Because this place has more to do with the acquisition and maintenance of power than with the pursuit of public good. And that's a huge tragedy.

Reg Alcock, Liberal MP, 1993–Present

I served both as a bureaucrat and a politician in the provincial legislature and I had a fair bit of access to information about what was going on at that level of government. The legislature plays a very direct role in overseeing the expenditures of government. In Ottawa, however, the system is so much bigger and it has become so ritualized that I think the House of Commons has lost a lot of its relevance in this regard. You can still do things if you're smart and you work hard, but the level of accountability that should exist is gone. The government has become so large and so complex, it's difficult to understand how it functions and it's too easy for MPs to be led astray by extraneous issues.

Donald Savoie, Author of *Governing from the Centre*

Sadly, accountability for the raising and spending of public funds falls virtually nowhere today. You have to understand that (a) MPs have no resources, and (b) we're dealing with a budget of $170 billion. For a member of Parliament, within a few weeks, to get a handle on that budget, to have an appreciation of what's being planned, is an impossible task. Unless we equip members of Parliament with the proper resources to go through all these numbers, to go through all these programs, I think we're whistling in the wind.

Jason Kenney, Canadian Alliance MP, 1997–Present

The single most important power of Parliament is the power of the purse. In parliamentary history we spent years fighting the Crown, literally fighting the Crown, to secure the power of the purse and protect commoners from an overly greedy monarch. Now the monarch is an executive branch of government and it has the power to bring forward legislation that raises taxes, changes tax rates and dramatically changes people's economic circumstances. Those of us who are in power, who have the responsibility of protecting the people and making sure that there aren't mistakes in the legislation, don't have the time or expertise to do so. We have to trust the bureaucrats. Essentially the permanent government — the bureaucracy — drafts, writes, manages and edits this whole enormous field of tax legislation which has a huge impact on people's daily lives.

Who are these folks? The bureaucracy, civil servants. And I'm sure they are good, well-intentioned, honest folk who are paid less then they probably would be in the private sector.

They're in a pretty difficult position, too. They're given the job of managing this incredible power, this tax legislation that can make or break people economically. They work in some office tower as I do, the finance building here in Ottawa, but I don't know who they are. I might see them once or twice a year when I'm getting a briefing. They act in the name of the minister of finance, with the authority of the minister, and really we all have to trust them.

I'll tell you, on issues like tax legislation the only folks who really know what's going on are lobbyists for particular industries. A lot of the tax legislation deals with particular industries and particular sectors of the economy. For example, a bill may deal with oil and energy industry taxation, or taxation in the motion picture industry. Experts in those fields will come in and lobby directly the third-ranking person in the tax division of the Department of Finance as to what they want to be in the bill. To tell you the truth, that's where the real decisions are made. They're not made in the House of Commons, and certainly not made in the Senate. They're made between technical experts representing particular industries and bureaucrats who are part of the permanent government. Their consensus is dropped on us parliamentarians.

Theoretically all this legislation goes through with the approval of the minister who represents the government, and then with the approval of Parliament. But I can tell you, the minister doesn't understand the technical aspects of some of this legislation any better than the layman.

George Baker, Liberal MP, 1974–2002

Members of Parliament no longer debate money bills. No longer is the executive held accountable for estimates or even the money vote. About 20 years ago the Conservative government was defeated on a money bill with a vote of no confidence. A precedent was set when the House changed our procedures to prevent that from happening again. You can't have a government where bills are defeated.

The auditor general says that the role of MPs is to be the guardians of the public purse. But if they can't hold the government accountable for very basic things like money bills or estimates, how can they fulfill that role?

Donald Savoie, Author of *Governing from the Centre*

Accountability is important in the raising and spending of public funds because it is to citizens what market share is to the private sector. It's the only way we really know if things work out the way they ought to work out, or if something that was done was not appropriate. To hold people to account is to determine if they have done what they said and to ensure they haven't played fast and loose with the public funds.

There are all kinds of examples of a lack of accountability in spending money that I can share with you, depending on the prime minister. Jean Chrétien, for example, we now know that the $2 billion he put into the Millennium Scholarship Fund was something that he designed with a few key advisors. They decided to run it by Finance Minister Paul Martin to make sure that money will be put aside. Cabinet learned of the $2-billion expenditure no sooner than you or I did. It was the prime minister's initiative. He decided on the program's scope and ran with it. Now, is he accountable? Members of Parliament can ask questions in the House of Commons, and he'll answer as best he can or as best as he wants. Is that accountability? I don't think so. I think we've concentrated those decisions too much into the hands of too few.

One ongoing problem MPs spoke of is how overwhelming the task is of overseeing a $170-billion organization like the federal government. The federal government is like a labyrinth. It has dozens of ministries, hundreds of departments and agencies and over 100,000 employees. The budget books that MPs are assigned to read are literally thousands of pages long. There is no doubt MPs on the government side as well as in the opposition parties feel understaffed and overworked in this regard.

Jason Kenney, finance critic for the Canadian Alliance, put into perspective what he is up against in trying to hold the government accountable for its spending actions.

Jason Kenney, Canadian Alliance MP, 1997–Present

I'm the principal spokesman and ombudsman for the 60 percent of Canadians who didn't vote for the government. As finance critic in the Opposition, my job is to keep track of the fiscal and economic policies of the government. I have to deal with any legislation dealing with taxation that comes before the House.

For example, we have a 1,400-page tax code and every now and then the government comes to Parliament with complex amendments to this Byzantine tax code that literally nobody in the country fully understands. I only have a staff of a couple of people, and I'm up against a department with thousands of employees, including expert economists and technical experts in drafting legislation and taxation.

A couple of months ago the government tabled a 500-page bill of technical amendments to the Income Tax Act and a bunch of other tax statutes. I think they gave us about 36 hours' notice to decide what our position was going to be and how we were going to vote. I have one staff member who does legislation for me, who is already working 14-hour days. We don't have the budget or the technical lawyers to get into this sort of thing. So essentially MPs, particularly on the government's side, but even opposition MPs, have to take the government at its word that legislation like this works. I would say probably about a quarter of this legislation is actually fixing mistakes they've made in past legislation.

The bureaucrats responsible for drafting bills come to the finance minister and say, "We need to pass this legislation for these reasons." The minister doesn't read the legislation, he doesn't understand it, he just introduces it in the House. I, as the Opposition critic, don't have time to delve into it. I get a general sense of what's in there, decide whether our party is for it or against it and try to make some general points in the debate. That's the process. It's absolutely ridiculous. I mean, I actually asked the finance minister if I could get a briefing on this bill. He said, "Sure, if you can figure out what it's all about, let me know."

This is the madness of Parliament.

We're talking about the tax power, which next to the criminal law power is the single most destructive and coercive power that Parliament can wield. We can make or break people economically. We can take away the fruits of their labour. We can violate their property rights. We can do all of that through this tax legislation. There isn't a single member of Parliament who will have read this bill before it's passed, but they'll all vote on it. That's what's wrong.

I suspect most readers will see that Jason Kenney is referring to more than just tax legislation. Sure, one line of tax code alone can change how much money we can put in our RSPs, or how high the capital gains tax will be when we sell our cottages or mutual funds. Indeed, every line of the tax code affects Canadians in one way or another. The point that should be taken from his remarks is that every piece of legislation passed by Parliament, whether or not it is tax legislation, entitles the government to act. And every action taken by Parliament affects us, usually hitting us in our pocketbooks sooner or later.

So if MPs are not keeping an eye on things, how do citizens know if the crank (government) is attached to the wheel that directs it (Parliament)? The fact is we don't. In most instances this cause and effect between the laws passed by our Parliament and the government's power to act is lost. As citizens and voters we need to feel confident our MPs, and the government itself, are looking after our interests.

John Williams, Reform and Canadian Alliance MP, 1993–Present[2]

Taxes are important to Canadians. They are being spent by the ton, all $170 billion per year of them. Yet this spending goes through the House of Commons in a flash. We approved $170 billion worth of expenditures and we didn't analyze one department or one program in depth at all.

As MPs we are given a stack of documents and that is only the summary of the spending. When you open that, you see a summary, an infrastructure program — $2.5 billion — you can't ask an intelligent question probing what the infrastructure program is all about. You only have one line — $2.5 billion. What does that represent?

So when it comes to numbers — $170 billion and stacks of budget books all over the place — MPs' eyes glaze over and there's an, "Oh, I don't understand that. I'm glad you're looking after it for me." MPs say they don't look after spending because they see me, John Williams, trying to look after it. But one MP can't do it. I can't analyze $170 billion by myself, nor can I, as the chair of the Public Accounts Committee with 17 members, analyze all that money. It requires a majority in the House of Commons. It requires 151 MPs or more. The problem is they're all off on their own tangents.

You start investigating some sort of spending program and the MP sitting next to you says, "Oh, I'm not interested in infrastructure programs. I'm interested in pensions for seniors." So you get no support from him to follow on your line for infrastructure investigation because he's waiting to get the microphone so he can ask about pensions. When he gets to pensions somebody else says, "Oh, no, I don't want to talk about pensions. I want to talk about the fact that our military is falling apart." So MPs are talking about defence, environment, taxes or seniors' pensions because that is their individual focus, but Canadians don't get an orchestrated, concentrated, ongoing investigation on any one spending program because every MP has their own pet projects.

The process is so complex; people don't understand the process by which spending goes through the House. They say, "Let's go home. Somebody's looking after the store, hopefully." But there isn't anybody looking after the store. They vote yes and they go home. The next year we return and the government doesn't even tell us how they've spent the money.

If we are going to get the authority back into Parliament, it requires a majority of parliamentarians, which means getting some government members to say, "We have got to bring the authority back into this place." And that's not easy.

Peter Dobell, Director, The Parliamentary Centre

Accountability of public spending hasn't been very effective for the past 50 years. But it is certainly ineffective now.

One of the biggest failings of Parliament today is that it never really has been very successful at reviewing how government spends money. Part of the problem is that government finance is now extraordinarily complex, so that you'd have to spend a great deal of time and have very large staffs to review it effectively. There is a feeling that it was better in the past because the Estimates had to be approved in the House and were debated in the House. But that ended in 1968. It had reached the point where Parliament was approving government expenditure one month at a time. It had become a system for holding up the government until the last moment, but always paying it at the last moment. Quite often the only thing they'd get is that one department would have some cuts made to it. It wasn't a very thoughtful analysis of how the money was spent.

Scott Brison, Progressive Conservative MP, 1997–Present

It's important to remember that before the late 1960s departmental spending estimates were debated here on the floor of the House of Commons by the Committee of the Whole, where all parliamentarians were part of the debate. That has changed and that change has had a very deleterious impact on the degree to which individual members of Parliament can contribute to public policy, the development of programs and prioritizing spending.

Bill Blaikie, New Democratic MP, 1979–Present

One of the roles of a member of Parliament is to act as a guardian of the public purse. It's the spending and taxing aspect of the job. It's also a question of policy, too. What is the government spending? Is it spending it wisely or not? But also there's the policy aspect, as in what is the government doing to address various problems.

Now, the spending of government is very hard to examine in a truly investigative way because it's the committees to which the spending estimates are referred, but the committees are under the thumb of government. It's extremely difficult to use committees in the way that they ought to be used, to really give the government a hard time, in the sense of scrutinizing government activity both on the expenditure side and on the policy side.

Joe Clark, Progressive Conservative Leader and Former Prime Minister

Parliament's not working at all. It hasn't been working for a long time. One mistake all parties made about 35 or 40 years ago occurred when we ended a system in which there could be control of spending by something called Committee of the Whole. Parliament was once able to debate spending proposals as long as it wanted, and until Parliament said yes the government could not spend a cent. That system obviously could be abused and it was changed. However, once Parliament lost its control of spending, it lost its control of the government because the only way you can control any government is through their spending power. What we have to do is bring in a system in which we restore that previous kind of control over spending by the Parliament.

Paul Dick,
Progressive Conservative MP, 1972–1993, and Former Cabinet Minister
The principal change took place in 1969, when they stopped doing the Estimates in the House of Commons in what was called the Committee of the Whole. It had been a way of slowing down government by tying up the Estimates for day after day. As a result the government couldn't pass their legislation.

In the first year of the Trudeau administration they changed the rules of the House of Commons by invoking closure, and they moved the Estimates into committees outside the House — the standing committees. They also changed the rules so that committee members could discuss the Estimates and vote on them, but if they did not vote on them by June 23, then the Estimates would be deemed to have passed.

As soon as they deemed the Estimates to have passed, everybody lost interest in them. As a result the committee members started to argue about policy at the standing committees, but they no longer discussed the finances of a department. That's when we lost public scrutiny of Parliament. Nobody was counting the beans anymore. Nobody was taking a look at what was happening with the dollars and cents.

Scott Brison, **Progressive Conservative MP, 1997–Present**
I'm particularly critical of current budgetary issues. In 2001 Paul Martin and the Liberal government made an arbitrary and irresponsible decision not to have a budget in that year. One of the most fundamental problems with not having a budget is that

individual members of Parliament are denied the opportunity to debate, discuss and ultimately vote on the spending of taxpayers' money. There is a historically unprecedented, near-toxic level of arrogance demonstrated by a government that decides on its own that it's doing things right and that Parliament does not deserve the respect of allowing individual members to debate, discuss, develop and vote on budget proposals.

When the rights and privileges of individual members of Parliament are denied to this extent, the rights of their constituents are also denied. This means that government spending follows the ruling party's desires and whims. It can be designed to appease backbenchers and it can be designed to appease the pet projects of Cabinet ministers. We've seen this happen in the past, in terms of the government taking Canadian taxpayers for granted and spending indiscriminately. But we've never seen the government do so without at least providing the opportunity for an effective debate in the House of Commons.

Jason Kenney, Canadian Alliance MP, 1997–Present

If anyone thinks MPs are a cornerstone of democracy regarding the public purse, they're being awfully naive because at best we are actors in a political theatre and from time to time can serve a useful purpose in terms of accountability. But most of the time we are spectators in a game which is controlled completely from inside government. And I say that as an Opposition member. I'm sure any honest government backbencher will admit that 100 percent of the power is in the Prime Minister's Office in our political system. The government backbenchers and opposition MPs are basically ordinary MPs, and they might theoretically be the bastions of democracy, but in practice the best we can do is ask questions, usually not get answers, and raise concerns that usually aren't listened to. While it sounds kind of cynical you still have to try because to give up on the system we have is basically to give up on democracy.

The role of Parliament and MPs to hold the government to account has been gradually diminished, especially with regard to the budget process, although the same is true of all parliamentary policy-making

135

processes. Many of our interviewees referred to a turning point in the late 1960s when Parliament began to lose control of the purse strings of government. During this decade the size and scope of government began to grow quickly. The 1962 Glassco Commission Report on Government Organization was an attempt to create a new management and oversight structure in government because it was felt government was starting to get too unwieldy and large for Parliament to control. The commission made many recommendations that would "let the managers manage government," giving individual bureaucrats more say and initiative over their own piece of the budget pie.

In its attempt to make the workings of government less unwieldy, the Glassco Commission Report inadvertently set the cat among the pigeons. Managers were not only managing; they began empire building. Managers' pay was based on the number of employees that reported to them: the more employees, the more clout and the more money they received. Government program spending went through the roof and the number of unelected people making decisions skyrocketed.

Parliament could not keep up with the demands of this growing government. When government was small and manageable, MPs could keep a handle on spending and programs, but when Parliament took away many of the controls governing bureaucratic departments without installing another set of controls, accountability went out the window. Not only was Parliament not asking what results government spending was achieving, most programs were not even costed-out to see whether they were affordable over the long run. When I interviewed former MP Paul McCrossan, who is a professional actuary, he recalled:

> One of the things that I found out personally in 1979 was that the Canada Pension Plan was the only social program for which we had any estimates in the long term at all. The Old Age Security had never been estimated for more than a year and a half in advance, as far as I can find out. The Guaranteed Income Supplement was never estimated until the late 1980s. To my knowledge the cost of medicare has never been estimated to this day. So we've brought in a lot of social programs figuring they were self-sustaining, but until 1986 nobody actually prepared the figures to determine if they could be afforded in the long run. We'd always gone on the basis that we can afford them.

The residue of that system remains. But how did Parliament and the MP's role become so diminished?

The Trudeau administration enacted legislation in 1968 that disabled the alarm system that should have warned MPs that their budget scrutiny role was in peril. The impact was profound and the role of the MP was central to the problem. Before 1968 all of Parliament was tasked with voting on government expenditures line by line. This process was called the Committee of the Whole because all of the budget matters were actually debated on the House of Commons floor. By the mid-1960s Parliament was being asked to vote on approximately 500 budget expenditures. Although this system could be cumbersome, it did allow *all* parliamentarians (whether or not they were members of the ruling party) to vote on and to debate expenditures.

The legislation, introduced in the name of time and efficiency, took the process of reviewing budgetary spending estimates away from the floor of the House of Commons and gave it to committees of Parliament, which were instructed to perform their review process on much tighter timelines. Opposition parties were also given far fewer days to hold the government to account, and as a result they were forced to pick and choose the issues they held dear. The number of days allotted to look at the business of supply (money estimates) was dropped to a total of 20 days, ending by June 23 of each year. Known as "Opposition Days," these 20 days were broken up into yearly time slots. During those days only eight votes could be held on budgetary items per day, with all other motions on the agenda for any particular day "deemed to have passed" by the end of that workday. If an issue was not discussed by 5:00 p.m. — too bad, it passed.

Various consequences have flowed from this new "pressure cooker" method of securing parliamentary approval. For government, clear benefits come from having a predictable financial calendar to follow. Government now knows that by June 23 of each year, whether Parliament has voted it or not, the government will receive the funds it wants because they would have been "deemed to have passed" as of that date. Opposition parties and backbenchers in many cases have come to believe, correctly, that they have lost most of their power as critics and scrutinizers of the government.

The opportunity for the public, through their supposed representatives, the MPs, to be heard on future budget priorities has all but vanished from our political system. The citizen is now completely out of the loop.

Since 1968 our politicians have been forced to consider budget estimates and policy priorities that are already set in stone for the next year, that are a fait accompli. The main estimates, which put the dollar figures to the broad policies of the ruling government, find their way through the various Public Accounts Committee structures *long after the budget year has already started.* To ensure the system rolls along unencumbered in the short run, a system of short-term appropriation bills are used. Appropriation bills are basically interim budgets passed by Parliament. In a debate of the House of Commons in 1994, Liberal House Leader Herb Gray summed up the problem of spending estimates: "The Estimates are complex to analyze and are, for constitutional reasons, difficult to change … As a result, the examination of main estimates has become cursory and there has been no focus for parliamentary debate on government spending before its spending priorities are set."

The implications of these shifts in parliamentary control of government spending are profound and go to the heart of how Canadians are governed. If the structures of our Parliament cannot adequately examine government expenditure proposals, parliamentarians are not fulfilling and cannot fulfill their constitutional duty.

Former MP and senator John Stewart witnessed first hand what has happened to this budget scrutiny. He was in the House of Commons in 1968 and saw how the intention of making Parliament more accountable led to its biggest failure.

John Stewart, Liberal MP, 1962–1968; Senator, 1984–1999

During the late 1960s I was an active member of an all-party committee that dealt with the reform of the rules of the House of Commons. There were various intentions to reforming the House, but I think the most important thing was to ensure that spending estimates were dealt with more adequately. At the time they were treated in a committee of the whole House, called the "committee of supply."

There were two things wrong with the old system. First, the Estimates were not being examined with the kind of detail they deserved. Second, the opposition, Liberals or Conservatives as the case might be, were using the Committee of the Whole to delay all the operations of the House. Most MPs today don't know really what it was like before 1968. Week after week there were trivial discussions of estimates in the chamber, with a relatively small number of members in the opposition asking questions. For example, back in 1962–63 the Diefenbaker government was still asking for supply for that fiscal year at the beginning of February 1963.

So we wanted a better process. Our report concluded it would be best to send the Estimates for each individual department or branch to an appropriate standing committee, then give the opposition a predetermined number of days in the House of Commons to deal with supply business. That was the scheme of the reform.

It wasn't a unilateral change; it was a unanimous decision of the House of Commons in the fall of 1968. Where previously supply business was dealt with by the committee of supply, a committee of the whole House of Commons, now the estimates for each department — Agriculture, Fisheries and so on — would be sent to a committee which dealt with agriculture, fisheries and so on. The idea was that there would be much more intensive examination of the Estimates because the committees would be composed of people who knew something about agriculture or fisheries and so on. They could get away from the general discussions that characterized the old committee of supply.

The outcome of the 1968 changes is rather disappointing; the outcome did not match the intent. The work of the committees is not what we hoped it would be. We were hoping that putting fairly expert members of Parliament to analyze the estimates of departments such as Agriculture, Fisheries or Foreign Affairs would result in close examination of government policy. We had hoped it would enable the ordinary members of Parliament to influence future policy. My impression is that the members of Parliament have not given much attention to government spending estimates since that time. The reforms didn't engage the vast number of backbenchers as intensively as we would have liked.

I think it is a well-accepted impression that the committees have *not* gone into the non-partisan examination of public policy in the way we had hoped. Intensive discussion of particular policies by expert members of Parliament is lacking, and that is a disappointment. In many instances they are not transmitting to the ministers the proposals for improvement in government policies and performance. One thing we have to remember is that an awful lot of the members of the House of Commons are there for a relatively short time, so they do not catch on to what opportunities the rules and procedures give them. Perhaps we expected too much from them.

With the system operating the way John Stewart describes it, is it any wonder that large debts and deficits were not addressed from the 1970s until the late 1990s? Or that in 2000 billions of dollars went missing from the budget of Human Resources Development Canada (HRDC) without an accounting of its whereabouts or what it was used for? Or that, as the Canadian Tax Foundation reported in February 2002, Canadian taxation is at its highest level in history? These things are hardly surprising if Parliament cannot or does not oversee how money is spent.

The main reason Parliament runs into difficulties overseeing money is that there is little or no regard for money *before* it is spent in our system. Once the political wheels are in motion, the inertia of government just keeps it going. Once the money is spent, Parliament has a tough time stopping it, redirecting it or correcting it.

To understand just how precipitous the decline of MPs' interest in overseeing the money Parliament authorizes has been, let us trace the deterioration since 1968. Between 1968 and 1972 all committees were expected to look at their own programs and make recommendations to the House of Commons about spending. After 1972 that power of recommendation was taken away. Part of the problem lay in the fact that the committee members could suggest reductions in spending but did not have the power to suggest increases. With the power of recommendation removed, the committees were relegated to bystander status.

In 1993 a liaison committee of Parliament composed of all the chairpersons of the permanent committees of Parliament observed:

As a result of the 1968 decision to transfer estimates from Committee of the Whole to standing committees, Canadian MPs in a majority Parliament have effectively lost the power to reduce government expenditure. Members are therefore making the very rational calculation that there is no point devoting time and effort to an exercise over which they can have no influence.

According to information provided by the Committees Branch of the Clerk's Office of the House of Commons, in 1990–1991, 20 permanent committees of Parliament held a total of 101.5 meetings on the spending estimates, but the committees produced *no* reports on these estimates back to the House. In 1991–1992, 20 committees held a total of 20 estimates meetings, but produced *only one* report. Skip ahead to 1997–1998. Twenty permanent committees held a total of 18.5 meetings on the Estimates, but only three reports made it back to the House. (For reasons known only to itself, Parliament keeps track of percentages of meetings.) By 2000–2001, there were 37 meetings, and *no* reports were filed. And so far this year (2001–2002 figures incomplete) there have been 25 estimates meetings, with four reports sent to the House of Commons.

To put these figures into perspective, overall committees (those that do not look at spending) held a total of 1,782 meetings for the period 2000–2002. Those committees have issued 261 reports to Parliament on other matters, yet only four on spending. In other words, the spending estimates represented only a little over three percent of the total meetings — and less than one-quarter of one percent of the reports made. The House of Commons in the meantime voted to spend (including interest on the $540-billion national debt) over $350 billion in this period.

We discovered that two MPs who sit on the most important committee of Parliament that looks at spending, the Public Accounts Committee, have tried to remedy this distressing situation. Marlene Catterall and John Williams made vain attempts to create a report that would fix Parliament's failure to be accountable over spending.

Marlene Catterall, Liberal MP, 1997–Present; Current Government Whip

When I first came to Parliament I was appalled — I'm still not exactly delighted — by the way parliamentary committees deal with the spending estimates. It basically becomes a shooting gallery. The opposition's there to try and find a target in the Estimates that allows them to shoot at the minister and criticize the government. After nine years on municipal council in Ottawa I was used to very detailed, very thorough study of budgets, of what the problems were and what the long-range plans were. So

I found this sort of superficial consideration of spending estimates in the federal government to be of serious concern.

There's a continuing dissatisfaction with members of Parliament, and that to me indicated an ongoing need for a watchdog for Parliament — on the spending estimates process and where members of Parliament fit into that equation. I was a member of the Public Accounts Committee and we decided to create a subcommittee called the Subcommittee on the Business of Supply. I was the chairperson. It was something I asked to do because it's a subject that really interests me and that I think is of great public importance.

Our focus was in large part on how to put in place the measures that would enable parliamentary committees and individual MPs to have a stronger influence on public policy. So that's the fundamental principle of the Business of Supply report that we created out of that committee.[3]

John Williams, Canadian Alliance MP, 1993–Present

Understanding how government spends money is a complex issue. When I first came to Ottawa as an MP I kicked and screamed and made all kinds of noises about how we just voted on budgets and spending, but nobody analyzed them.

This caused the Subcommittee on the Business of Supply to be created by Marlene Catterall, several other MPs and myself. The goal was to look for better ways for Parliament to oversee how money is spent. Out of that came a report on the business of supply. That's what we call the Estimates and the budgets going through the House — the business of supply.

Marlene Catterall, Liberal MP, 1997–Present; Current Government Whip

Our primary objective in writing the Business of Supply report was to make MPs more aware of the whole package of tools at their disposal, to influence not only the immediate budget and the immediate spending plans but longer-term, shifting priorities of the government, then to hold the government accountable for doing what it said it would do.

Some people look at the internal auditors as the enemy, there to find out your faults. I regard the auditor function as the biggest assistance government has in terms of finding out how well we are doing, how well the resources are being used, whether we're getting the results we should be getting and so on.

John Williams, Reform and Canadian Alliance MP, 1993–Present

The report we created was about 100 pages long and had 15 major recommendations, including the creation of an estimates committee to focus on spending all year round. The Public Accounts Committee (which I chair) is only a retrospective, rearguard look at what went wrong. We wanted an estimates committee to look at budgets *before* moneys are spent.

The report also recognized that Parliament must look at the different kinds of government spending to look at things not currently being examined. For example, program spending, called statutory spending (or spending that happens every year), never comes before the House of Commons for a vote. A good example is employment insurance. I think we created the program in 1947. Back when we passed the legislation there was one little clause that said they would get the money they required. We voted in 1947 and never voted on that issue again and this is 2002. To put it in perspective, over $100 billion is spent on program spending that is not even voted on in the House.

Our report also wanted to set up an evaluation program so Canadians can see if they are getting value for money. It was based on four simple questions. First, we wanted to know what the program was designed to do because in many cases there isn't even a public policy attached to government programs. Currently we just spend the money and keep it circulating. Surely Canadians would hope that we should get some benefit for the money we're spending. Second, how well is the program doing? This isn't rocket science here, but the government just doesn't want to know the answer to how most of our programs are doing. They just spend the money. Third, we wanted to ask whether we are delivering the programs efficiently. Fourth, and related to the third, can we achieve the same or better results for our government dollar by delivering the program in a different way in a fast-changing technological world?

These are four questions the government currently does not ask.

Marlene Catterall and John Williams, who come from different political persuasions and parties, worked harmoniously together to write their report, The Business Of Supply: Completing the Circle of Control. Robert Marleau, clerk of the House of Commons from 1987 to 2001, described the report in *The Hill Times* as a "fine piece of work." If the report were adopted by Parliament, it would fundamentally change the way Parliament works because it would help restore at least some aspects of Parliament's lost scrutiny of spending.

Initially the report's submission to Parliament was stalled when Jean Chrétien called the 1997 election. The Catterall-Williams report was reintroduced on December 10, 1998, but never reached the floor of the House of Commons for a vote. Why? A letter from Government House Leader Don Boudria explained, "Members' time is already stretched with the workload of the current committee system." The idea of creating an estimates committee to look at spending before money was spent was deemed redundant to the "current situation."

John Williams tried again to have this "fine piece of work" voted upon by MPs after the 2000 election — but now without the help of Marlene Catterall, who had since been appointed to the Cabinet as government whip. He submitted it as a private member's bill and the report, after five years of arduous work, was finally deemed "votable." His motion would come before the House of Commons on March 12, 2002. The odds against having a private member's bill of this magnitude actually passed are very long. Williams knew that he would have to convince many of the governing Liberal Party MPs to vote for his motion. What John Williams and Marlene Catterall told us about the motion when we interviewed them just prior to the actual vote was full of political intrigue.

John Williams, Reform and Canadian Alliance MP, 1993–Present

On our committee, we had a unanimous report and all parties agreed to this great report. I will be introducing it in the House; it will be debated for three hours and voted upon.

Marlene Catterall and I were co-authors on this report; Marlene is the government whip and she supported it. I look forward to seeing what the government does under her direction when it comes to a vote in the House. I hope she gets back to this accountability issue that she supported so strongly back on our committee.

Marlene Catterall, Liberal MP, 1997–Present; Current Government Whip

Because the Business of Supply report I co-authored never was endorsed by Parliament, John Williams, who was vice-chair of the subcommittee, is putting forward a motion that the government immediately implement the recommendations of the Business of Supply report. And I think "immediately" is something that we knew wasn't going to happen when we wrote the report five years ago. This is an evolutionary process. Things have to develop over a period of time.

I think many of my colleagues are not aware of the report, but nonetheless behind the scenes it's moving things forward. The report, although never adopted by Parliament, was received very positively within the administration. The Treasury Board, for instance, spent a lot of effort on trying to improve reporting to Parliament. We helped move that along a little more quickly. We recommended more resources for committees so they could have more independent research and not rely as much on the government for information. The 2001 Speech from the Throne actually did that, inserting more resources into the Library of Parliament, the main tool that most committees use to get their research done.

If there's one recommendation that hasn't been implemented but is quite important, it's establishing an estimates committee on the spending estimates process.

John's motion will be debated and voted on in Parliament as a private member's bill. Normally as government whip I would take no role in private members' business because we've made it clear that for our members of Parliament, private members' business is free votes. However, having chaired the subcommittee that produced the report, this is what I'm going to speak on.

I'll be speaking against adopting the report.

I might have a little verbal shot at John about the facility of being in opposition and asking for things to be done immediately when one knows, practically, that that's simply not possible. I give John great credit for the work he's done on this. I still feel that one of our main jobs is to get members of Parliament to use the tools they now have at their disposal and to more completely hold the government accountable for its spending. But as one of the co-authors of the report, I will be voting against it.

It's not an irony. John and I worked very well together on that committee. John started out fairly simplistically, as opposition often does, thinking that all the problems could be solved if we only had free votes and if we didn't have restraints on members changing what's in the spending estimates.

John Williams, Reform and Canadian Alliance MP, 1993–Present

Having supported it in committee, you would think as a parliamentarian she (Catterall) would support it in the House. But if the Liberal government says, "We'll give that a thumbs down," and she capitulates, folds and says, "OK, we're all going to give it a thumbs down," that clearly demonstrates why Parliament has lost its effectiveness. They can say something in committee and then they have to exercise the government's agenda, not Parliament's agenda. They change their tune and that's the end of it.

The deck is stacked against any one individual member, like myself, bringing accountability into Parliament. Parliament has allowed its authority to go to the government, and therefore the deck is stacked against Parliament as well.

Is it not ironic that Marlene Catterall planned to vote against her own report? It certainly seemed illogical that the champion and author of a new way of involving MPs in overseeing the most important piece of government business, spending, would change her tune as soon as she was given a Cabinet position by the prime minister. It makes one wonder whether the deck is stacked against *anyone* trying to hold the government accountable for spending, not to mention keeping the government and the executive — the prime minister and Cabinet — in check.

On the same day John Williams's motion was being voted upon by Parliament, March 12, 2002, a phone call came in from my colleague Jay

Innes, who attended the vote and witnessed the government handing out letters to Liberal MPs urging them to vote against the bill. In spite of these tactics and to my great surprise, Williams upset the apple cart. He managed to squeak out a tight victory of 112 votes for to 103 votes against, with 24 Liberals voting against their own party. Catterall's troops couldn't beat Williams, who successfully persuaded many Liberals away from their own party line — a rarity in our political system, especially when a bill has such weighty consequences for the government. Enough backbenchers saw that if they voted for this bill, their own relevance in the House of Commons would increase.

It is interesting to note that Liberal member Dr. Rey Pagtakhan, who voted *for* the Catterall-Williams bill in committee, voted *against* Williams's private member's bill on March 12, 2002. Between the initial drafting of the Catterall-Williams report and the parliamentary vote, Dr. Pagtakhan was promoted to Cabinet as minister of veterans affairs.

Money — who controls it and how it is allocated — is the biggest issue facing our Parliament. If Parliament can control the money, it can control the government. Currently that is not the case — far from it. Let us hope that there are more John Williamses who will fight the good fight in the future to bring about change.

An interesting postscript to this political drama between John Williams and Marlene Catterall was reported in a front-page article of the *National Post* on May 28, 2002. It reported that Williams's idea of creating an estimates committee which would do the job of scrutinizing money, a job that other parliamentary committees are *supposed* to do but are currently not performing, had just been passed by a vote in the House of Commons. In referring to the newly created committee, officially named the Committee on Government Operations and Estimates, Mr. Williams stated, "It improves the government's accountability and broadens the mandate of Parliament to look into issues it should have been looking at all along." But then Mr. Williams more cautiously added, "If allowed to work, this committee has the potential to influence government spending right across the board and the effectiveness of program delivery."

Perhaps there is some small hope for a better system, but it would seem that it is not a stretch to conclude that Mr. Williams, by cautioning that the committee will improve accountability only if it is "allowed to work," is hinting that something more insidious and systemic may encumber this new committee's effectiveness. The question is whether the new estimates committee will be any more effective than other adversarial and highly partisan parliamentary committees. Or, as the next chapter of this book explores, will Williams's committee simply fall victim to the same political pitfalls as the other 20 current permanent committees of Parliament? Only time will tell.

This final quote from John Stewart reminds us all what the consequences are to citizens if decisions concerning money are not properly scrutinized by Parliament.

John Stewart, Liberal MP, 1962–1968; Senator, 1984–1999

Voting money for the government is essential to the system. If members of the House of Commons and backbenchers on both sides are not exercising their control, the executive government (the prime minister and Cabinet), through no fault of its own, goes unchecked. Then mistakes made by ministers and bureaucrats in past performance are not detected and made public, and the programs for the future can't be improved without the input of members of Parliament.

Voters ought to be very concerned if members of Parliament are not precisely following what is being done with their money, which is supposed to be spent to provide good programs to the people of Canada. First, it's the taxpayers' money that is spent. Second, it is being spent on programs. Almost every taxpayer in the country has a real interest in assuring that those programs are as sound as they can be and as well administered as is possible. Parliament could absolutely not carry on without supply. Supply has to be voted to the government at least once a year. It is voted only one year at a time and it is the main means by which the responsibility of the executive government to the House of Commons, and thus to the people of Canada, is enforced.

Without money there are no programs. It's very important that members of Parliament scrutinize those programs. Otherwise we could be spending a lot of money and not getting adequate return in the form of good health care, support for our fisheries or agriculture — you name it. Parliament's job is to scrutinize the supply business and make sure that those programs are sound and are properly administered. There could be major improvements, but I think there are fundamental problems that make it very difficult for MPs to perform this essential duty.

NOTES

1. See the Web site of the Office of the Auditor General at http://www.oag-bvg.gc.ca/.
2. John Williams is also chairman of the Standing Committee on Public Accounts, or Public Accounts Committee (PAC), which oversees government spending.
3. The full name of the report was The Business of Supply: Completing the Circle of Control.

CHAPTER 7

The Fall of Committees:
Caged Tigers with No Teeth

As we witnessed in the last chapter, the supervision over the money spent by the Canadian Parliament is ineffectual at best. Parliament has just about abdicated its constitutional responsibility to ensure the $170 billion it spends annually is spent wisely for the proper purposes. Many of interviewees we spoke to made it clear that the failure of the parliamentary committee system is responsible for Parliament's weakness.

Most citizens are unaware just how important committees are to how Parliament works. Committees are the linchpins that tie the laws and bills that are passed in the House of Commons together with how our MPs influence government on behalf of their constituents. Committees are made up of groups of parliamentarians, selected from the Senate, the House of Commons or both, who deliberate on bills that are referred to them by either chamber after first reading. The House of Commons delegates most of the detailed study of proposed legislation and the scrutiny of government programs to its committees. Committees can also initiate reports and draft bills for consideration by Parliament.

A turning point in the committee system occurred in 1968, when the examination of the government's spending estimates was moved out of the House of Commons into the committees, thereby dramatically increasing the level of committee activity. Ideally this meant that more power was being delegated to the individual MPs who served on these busy committees, and it was thought that they would have more influence, not less. Paradoxically, the exact opposite situation has evolved from this change. As former MP and senator John Stewart said in an interview:

> My impression is that the committees have not gone into the non-partisan examination of public policy in the way that we had hoped. There is not that intensive discussion of particular policies by expert members of Parliament … That has been lacking, and it is a disappointment.

This was not an uncommon complaint among our interviewees. But why are committees of Parliament such a disappointment? Why is this most meaningful vehicle for MPs to flex their legislative muscle not living up to its potential?

Because every MP in Parliament sits (or has sat) on various committees, they have differing views about these questions. I spoke to approximately 30 MPs, as well as to various students of Parliament about this matter. To sum up their responses, MPs tend to "stand where they sit," as the old saying goes. In other words, their views depend on what party they belong to or on which position they hold on a committee. Nevertheless, I think it is fair to say that negative views of our system far outweigh positive ones. Not surprisingly, MPs who are in the Cabinet express the most positive views of the system.

Marlene Catterall, Liberal MP, 1997–Present; Current Government Whip

Committees are the heart and soul of parliamentary work. I know everybody focuses on Question Period for 45 minutes every day. But in fact the bulk of work of parliamentarians gets done in their committees. There's one attached to every department, and there are some special committees that aren't related to departments of government. But that's where members work together, and if it's a good committee, members tend to put aside their partisan differences and really work on the issues that are of concern to them.

Rahim Jaffer, Canadian Alliance MP, 1997–Present

Everyone has something to add to the debate, and I think deep down all the members in Parliament, no matter what party they belong to, they've all got the greater good in mind; they all want to do the best that they possibly can. Unfortunately we all disagree on the way to get to that final good and that's a challenge, to see if we can come up with a consensus.

As an opposition MP, if you've got a good relationship in committee then maybe you can affect the way other MPs think. But obviously you still have a majority party on the other side of the committee that makes the final decisions, so there's no guarantee after those changes are made in committee that they'll actually be adopted by Parliament.

The biggest frustration is the fact that even though you may have some good ideas, even though you might have something positive to add, as an opposition MP you have a little bit of influence but absolutely no power, and that's, I think, the most frustrating part of it. Because you can influence the process at times, but really at the end of the day you cannot affect the decision.

Dennis Mills, Liberal MP, 1988–Present

There's a lot of fantastic work by committee members that very rarely sees the light of day. By and large, the media do not cover those committees' meetings, so they miss a lot of issues of vital interest to the people of Canada, and the public doesn't get an accurate reflection of the passion, quality and commitment of many members of Parliament.

Reg Alcock, Liberal MP, 1993–Present

Committee work is a big issue around here. Committees actually have enormous power, and I have a desire to see committees assuming responsibilities and the authority that they currently have but do not use.

Determining if you have a good or bad experience on committees depends on the committee, the budget and the other

152

members who sit on it. If MPs on committees were able to stay on a committee for the life of the Parliament, committees would increase their authority. If you get experienced members you can achieve a lot. But if the committee becomes highly partisan, just fighting all the time and not discussing issues, then it becomes a waste of time.

Committees should challenge, question and search for the right answers from the minister. If the situation becomes politicized, the whips can drive it so that the government members defend the minister instead of being part of the process of holding the government accountable.

Scott Brison, Progressive Conservative MP, 1997–Present

I'm on the industry committee and finance committee, but more active in the finance committee, as vice-chairman. I have been able to work co-operatively with other members of opposition, particularly on the finance committee, which is an exponentially more functional committee than the industry committee, which is currently being operated by the chairperson as a branch plant of the minister of industry's office. She is his resident lap dog. So it's hard to form an effective committee with that sort of thing going on. But at the finance committee we have demonstrated that by being more effective parliamentarians, individually we can make a difference. The finance committee never submits a unanimous report. There is always a main report, which is written by the staff for the committee, and then there are dissenting reports by the opposition parties.

The fact is that the committee process has the potential to be accountable. However, many committees are being operated as branch plants of ministers' offices. That is not the intention of committees. Currently back-bench members in the Liberal government are not given the level of opportunity to express the views of their constituents or their own views on policy issues.

Don Boudria,
Liberal MP, 1984–Present; Current Government House Leader

The quality of work that Canadian parliamentary committees do is envied by people in other countries. Our parliamentary committees here witness about 90 percent of the legislation introduced in the House of Commons. We go through bills clause by clause. Sometimes dozens and dozens of amendments are produced to improve the legislation so that the bill comes back to the House better. In countries such as the U.K., for instance, they will routinely adopt bills in committee without listening to one witness. Nobody comes. Occasionally a government minister will come, testify and then that's it. Our system, I think, works much better. I really compliment the members of Parliament who work on parliamentary committees. They do very good work.

I realize some MPs say that power has been removed from the legislature and committees. People cannot say that MPs have less power now than they used to. I believe that that is not correct. They might crave or want — and that's a normal aspiration — more power. Everyone wants to be in Cabinet and so on. That's all OK. But it's not the same as saying that they have less power than they did, say, 10 years or 20 years ago. As a matter of fact, I would argue that MPs have a lot more influence now.

Keith Martin, Reform and Canadian Alliance MP, 1993–Present

Committees are just a show for the public to give the illusion that Parliament is working and that citizens' concerns are being listened to. But citizens' concerns are not being heard, and that is really sad. It's a big sham.

I can give examples of my personal experience in committees. I am a physician, and one of the reasons I came to Parliament was to save our publicly funded health-care system. People are dying on our waiting lists. Many people suffer in silence in the community, denied access to health care. So what have we done in the health committee over the last nine years? We have not touched the issue of how to save our public system. Rather, we have proceeded to deal with cigarettes and plain packaging. We talk about Aboriginal mental health. As important as these issues are, why study Aboriginal mental health when a royal commission report has just been done — $60 million — on all aspects of Aboriginal health and other issues affecting Aboriginal people? Committees need to focus on the issues facing all Canadians.

All of the citizen and MP interventions that are made in committee go into a big black hole, forgotten and never implemented. We recently met to discuss the Free Trade Agreement of the Americas, just two weeks before the meeting in Quebec. A member of the public offered a very eloquent comment, asking, "Why are you having this meeting only two weeks before the actual meeting?" And the answer is, the public is not meant to have constructive input into the debate or affect the happenings at that meeting.

We have many good, competent, honest, hard-working members of Parliament sitting on committees, but their good work is being deliberately tossed away and forgotten by a government that just wants to use committees as a make-work project for MPs. Worse, the heartfelt submissions by members of the public to these committees are not used either. So citizens are cut out of the loop as well. That is a real tragedy. It's a waste of human potential.

Suzanne Tremblay, Bloc Québécois MP, 1993–Present

Committees sometimes get their paperwork at the last minute. Everything we have to read and all the stuff we have to go through is a real problem and often we lack basic information. For instance, once, in the Canadian heritage committee, we knew a little bit about the problem before us, but we did not have even a minimum of information and were hearing some things for the first time as the committee chairperson read them.

We can do committee research ourselves, but we often don't have the time to do it. It's the kind of situation in which we may get a general report one day when the committee meeting is the next. It's impossible to go through everything to ask questions to the government.

From what I've heard it's always been like this, kind of a tradition. It's very rare that we have documents with enough time in advance to make up our mind on matters, so sometimes we have to speak about things that we know little about. If we discover something that concerns us, we will speak to it, but chances are we will miss it.

Also, there are times when we have to get involved with bills in areas other than our main subject. For example, the minister of finance had a bill called C-44, which was a very big bill that we wanted changed by the Finance Department. We found about halfway through the bill an article that obviously didn't look very important to people in the Finance Department, but it introduced what we called an "ejection seat" for the chairs of the CBC, Telefilm Canada and the National Film Board. We had to deal with that issue, but it's quite difficult for an MP to go through all this stuff.

It's difficult to know exactly what the best way to do committee work is. Members often feel that if we question in committee, it is sometimes seen as boring or stupid. We don't want to look stupid, so sometimes we don't ask the basic questions that could be important. It's not always easy, but of course we are ordinary people and we do the best we can.

Marlene Catterall, Liberal MP, 1997–Present; Current Government Whip

A piece of legislation is never a fait accompli when it comes to a committee. You just have to look at the record of how committees have dealt with legislation, have made substantial changes to legislation. Liberal as well as opposition members have put forward amendments to legislation that are accepted, and they're often the result of discussions among Liberals themselves, who say, "Hey, we think legislation needs to be changed in this way or that way." But that can also happen with opposition members.

I've served in opposition, too, so I can speak from both sides of the House. If you've really got something that you think makes sense, you can usually persuade the government that it makes sense and that a piece of legislation should be changed. You sit down, you meet with the officials, you meet with the ministry, you meet with the minister's parliamentary secretary, you do your homework.

Judy Wasylycia-Leis, New Democratic MP, 1997–Present

I feel good about at least being part of the committee process, proposing amendments and getting them on the record, actually sometimes getting amendments approved. At the same time one of my biggest disappointments in Parliament has also been the committee system. I was told that this would be the one place to get beyond partisanship and to truly get down to some hard work to develop good public policy for Canadians. It doesn't work that way. The party lines are clearly drawn in committee and the government cracks the whip. Our powers are very limited.

I have been frustrated for years as the one NDP member on the health committee because it has been totally controlled and manipulated by the government and unable to set an agenda based on the concerns of the people. We have a minister of health who comes in and tells us what our priorities are. Do you think the health-care crisis is on the agenda, or the future of medicare? Not a chance. This is a good indication of how dysfunctional Parliament has become, and I think there is now enough dissatisfaction that we can actually demand some changes. MPs from all parties are now talking about this because it affects us all.

Time and time again MPs told me that their most important way of influencing things was through committees but that committees don't work. These MPs appeared to be afflicted with a sort of "dual personality" disorder that probably acts as a defence mechanism against having to confront their lack of power over government.

In justifying their roles as our elected representatives (and their relevance to our whole political system, for that matter), MPs repeated how demanding and hard their work is, while complaining that they aren't listened to or heard. I started to wonder whether all this "busy work," as some of the MPs themselves called it, was for naught. Why do we have a committee system at all? Under the current system, if the committees simply rubber-stamp legislation the government has already decided upon, and then Parliament simply votes for whatever the ruling party proposes, then why bother with a committee system?

The answer to these questions is fairly simple: the system as it runs now is not how it is supposed to run. Parliament and its institutions, including the committee system, are supposed to be an inherent check on government. These places are where an MP's influence is supposed to rest and where power is supposed to be dispersed away from the centre.

Close study of this most important institution of Parliament shows that the committee system started to decline in relevance during the late 1960s.

Peter Dobell, Director, The Parliamentary Centre

It was the case in the 1960s that a committee received what is called an "order of reference" from the government, indicating that they would like the committee's views on that subject. So when the members were working on an issue, they felt that what they were doing was going to be listened to. And indeed they were. Now there isn't the same focus on issues. There is less of a sense that the government is interested in having their views.

Nowadays the government already has its agenda set. In the past the government would assign issues to committees and listen to their recommendations. Today the committee decides on its own agenda. That's the first problem. The second problem is that the issues come to committee when the government has already made up its mind on issues, and so the members on the committee from the government side feel compelled to follow the party line.

If you can change the dynamic, if you create a condition where the government members don't feel they have to defend what has already been endorsed by the government, that would also free up the opposition members on the committee. They wouldn't always feel they have to oppose the government because there would be no set government policy to attack.

George Baker, Liberal MP, 1974–2002

In 1968 changes to Parliament, specifically the powers taken away from the ordinary member of Parliament on the floor of the House of Commons, were supposed to be compensated for in the committees.

The committees were empowered to bring experts in so that members could sink their teeth into issues, move forward and make suggestions. But that's not how the system has evolved. Now they're encumbered by terms of reference determined by the leaders in their party. In other parliamentary systems the committee has a lot of power and can originate its own terms of reference. This means that it can investigate whatever it wants to. It's a completely different ballgame. If a committee wanted, for example, to investigate medications for cancer patients, it could do so in Great Britain. It could do so in

158

Australia. But it couldn't move forward in Canada. We can't do anything that the government doesn't want. That's the way the system is set up.

John Stewart, Liberal MP, 1962–1968; Senator, 1984–1999

The outcome of the 1968 changes is rather disappointing. The work of the committees is not what we hoped it would be. We were hoping that putting fairly expert members of Parliament to analyze the estimates of departments such as Agriculture, Fisheries or Foreign Affairs would result in close examination of government policy. We had hoped it would enable the ordinary members of Parliament to influence future policy.

I think it is a well-accepted impression that the committees have not gone into the non-partisan examination of public policy in the way we had hoped. Intensive discussion of policies by expert members of Parliament is lacking. I think one thing we have to remember is that an awful lot of the members of the House of Commons are there for only a short time. Many MPs do not catch on to what opportunities the rules and procedures give them.

I think it has a lot to do with the fact that the committees tend to be rancorous and that the time allotted to scrutinizing the government is divided between too many political parties. Committees only meet for a set amount of time each week, so when we have five or six political parties all asking different questions, it shatters the time available to a committee. It means committees are not performing as efficiently or with as much focus as they might if there were only two or three parties.

Also holding back committees is prime ministerial power, which does not like to be examined too intensively by backbenchers on either side of the House. I don't think the government has any zeal for careful scrutiny of its operations. This means that the members of Parliament in many instances are not transmitting to the ministers and to the bureaucracy proposals for improvement.

Finally, committee work does not get the kind of media coverage that a well-placed question, at Question Period, asked in the House of Commons would get. To some extent what is

happening is a result of the fact that the media tends to con-
centrate on Question Period. Question Period has become the
House of Commons for the media and for the members of
Parliament, not the committees anymore.

Peter Dobell, Director, The Parliamentary Centre

Part of the problem in committees is that the media pays very
little attention to committees unless a minister is in trouble and
is going to be there. It used to be in the 1960s, and even into the
1970s, when a committee was meeting the media would be all
over it. It would get well publicized, so the members who were
participating would feel that they were making a contribution.

Bill Blaikie, New Democratic MP, 1979–Present

Part of the problem is that the role of Parliament hasn't
changed. It was weak in the 1980s, it was weak in the 1990s and
it's weak now in this new century. There is another long-running
frustration on the part of members of Parliament, generally,
that really goes back to the 1980s and before: the sense that
members of Parliament don't have the power that the people
who elect them think they have, or think they should have. And
so there have been various attempts at parliamentary reform to
try to give individual members of Parliament more power, as
individuals and collectively as members of committees.

What we were trying to do with the McGrath Committee (in
the 1980s) was strengthen both the independence of the individual backbenchers and strengthen the power of the House of
Commons against the Cabinet, the executive, the prime minister,
by strengthening the role of individual MPs. By strengthening
committees, it gives more independence to members, both collectively and individually. Since that time we've had very little
progress, but a few things have happened. There are more private
members' bills that come to a vote and that are sometimes passed.
But by and large the committees are as much under the thumb of
the government as they ever were. In fact worse in some cases.

And when committees are under the thumb of the government, then the spending of the government is very hard to
examine in a truly investigative way.

I conducted several in-depth interviews with Bill Blaikie, who is the NDP House leader and a parliamentary expert. Since first being elected in 1979 Blaikie has been the type of fellow who could speak on almost any issue affecting Parliament, as he has been a member of almost every committee that has looked at the issue of making Parliament work better. He has seen minor procedural changes over that time but, as he noted above, he believes little in the way of giving committees true influence has occurred.

The situation Blaikie describes of MPs being "under the thumb of government" brings up the issue of political party discipline and the intertwined relationship that exists in Canada between government and those who are elected to oversee it. At the risk of sounding like a drumbeat, I will reiterate this simple fact: Parliament's job is to oversee and check that the government is doing what it said it would do and to determine whether its actions are appropriate. A parliamentarian's job is to use the committee system and their votes on the floor of the House of Commons to ensure this happens. But the line between government and Parliament in Canada is hazy at best. As Liberal MP Reg Alcock has explained:

> Ministers represent their department. That's their role. So you would expect an adversarial relationship with the committee, in the sense that the committee should be challenging, questioning and searching for the right answers. If the situation becomes politicized, the whips can drive it so that the government members defend the minister instead of being part of the process.

We should not forget that ministers are the government but parliamentary committees are not the government. The committees are there to ensure that the ministers are on the right track, asking the right questions, demanding answers and ensuring that the departments they oversee are acting in the best interests of Canadians.

A frequent complaint of our interviewees was how the political party system and the partisanship it is based on has blurred this line between government and Parliament. One specific detrimental change to how committees operate occurred in April 1991, when parliamentary secretaries were permitted to become members of a committee. Why is this significant? The parliamentary secretary is a government party MP who is responsible for assisting a minister with various

House of Commons duties, including supervising the passage of the minister's proposed legislation through Parliament, attending outside events in the minister's absence and speaking for an absent minister during Question Period. In other words, the parliamentary secretary is no longer just an MP; he or she is now part of the government. So although a parliamentary secretary is not in a true power position, he or she now represents the government and has an active interest in defending the minister and the department, rather than in demanding that tough questions be answered. Parliamentary secretaries often find themselves in the dubious situation of having their positions and prospects defined by their loyalty to their minister. Parliamentary secretaries often become government enforcers on committees, keeping freethinkers in line.

Scott Brison, Progressive Conservative MP, 1997–Present

I still find that the degree to which committees are closely related, particularly by their chairpersons, to the ministers' offices is unfortunate. Being heavily weighted in favour of the government is not the intention behind committees and they're not functioning as effectively as they should.

Chuck Strahl, Reform and Canadian Alliance MP, 1993–Present

Every morning the government sets out to consciously deter innovative members of Parliament from contributing. For example, they put the parliamentary secretaries on the committees to make sure that the government agenda gets addressed, not the concerns of individual MPs or of individual committees. They make sure the parliamentary secretaries dictate to the committees what gets done there, what doesn't and what amendments are acceptable, what witnesses are acceptable and so on. It's just railroading of the committee process.

Ted McWhinney, Liberal MP, 1993–2000

I was a member of the foreign affairs committee, then parliamentary secretary. As a parliamentary secretary I was not just an MP, I was also a representative of the government. My job as a member of the committee was to communicate to the chairperson of the committee (who was always a member of my own

162

party — except in the case of the Public Accounts Committee). It was my obligation to communicate my government positions to the committee, as well as be a voting member of the committee. I'm not sure that it is a good plan constitutionally to have a minister, or his representative on behalf of the government, sitting on the same committee that is supposed to scrutinize his or her ministry.

Contrast ours to the American system. A member of the executive would never be a member of a congressional committee overseeing any part of the government.

The truth of the matter is that committees wield tremendous power to study issues and call witnesses, including the prime minister. But they choose not to use their power.

The problem lies in the committees' connection with the House of Commons. By now we know that everything that runs through the House of Commons is influenced heavily, and mostly to its detriment, by the party system. All the power flows back to the prime minister and Cabinet because of the power of party politics over the House of Commons. Considering that committee membership is directly proportional to each political party's percentage of seats in the House of Commons, it is not a big stretch to see that the prime minister's reach extends past the floor of the House of Commons right into the committees. Particularly when the prime minister, through his party whip, decides which MPs sit on which committees. If the prime minister wants a piece of legislation passed, the committees cannot stop it. The opposition can try to stall legislation, but those MPs on the government side will inevitably vote for it.

Currently MPs from the government side are stuck in a bind. Under our system MPs are supposed to hold the government to account, even if that means giving their own party (and the prime minister) a hard time once in a while. But the GST debates of the early 1990s, the gun-control debates of 1995–96 and the hepatitis C debate in 1999–2000 made it clear that the government sets the agenda and that MPs who disagree with the government's stance are forced to fall into line with it. The committees of Parliament were powerless to resist the government's will on these issues.

Canadians should also be troubled by how members of committees are being used as pawns in the chess game of party politics. The fact that the whips choose MPs to sit on committees based on their allegiance to their party leads one to question how much critical scrutiny an MP will give the government. But what I found most surprising was how MPs' talents were being squandered on committees. It often seems that MPs with expertise, analytical skills and a deep interest in a particular issue are being overlooked for committee membership simply because they do not adhere to their own political party's strict party line.

Also, the intentional — but often unnecessary — substitution of MPs as members of committees, and the gratuitous rotation of parliamentary secretaries, on average, every 18 months (as has been done since the time of Mackenzie King), along with the frequent shuffling of Cabinet ministers, makes little sense. Just as ministers start to gain the specialized knowledge they need to run their departments, they are moved to another portfolio. Two years in the life of a minister is not a long time when you bear in mind that the government and its civil servants are often in place for decades.

In the words of Liberal MP Peter Adams, who has served on several parliamentary committees, "The lack of institutional memory must be overcome. Should my minister and I find the key to the minister–parliamentary secretary relationship, it will be forgotten and lost as soon as my appointment is terminated."[1]

From a prime minister's managerial point of view, perhaps it makes sense to shuffle ministers frequently, for if no one is in a position long enough to gain an informed understanding of the issues in a department or ministry, there will be fewer challenges to the centralized power structure of government. The Privy Council Office, the Prime Minister's Office and the prime minister himself are able to keep tighter watch over potential flare-ups of resistance to their agenda. But from the citizen's point of view, lack of expertise in overseeing the government cannot be a good thing.

Ted McWhinney, Liberal MP, 1993–2000

Because how our Parliament operates is tied into this British parliamentary executive, the committee system is weak and ineffectual. The party whips control the membership of committees. I don't know how often they organize their talent banks and see what resources are available. You find people ending up on committees because they go to the government whip and ask to be put on, not because they are necessarily expert in the field, but because the committee has a large travelling budget, which allows MPs to travel to exotic places. Foreign affairs is a prized committee because it has a lot of money for travel, and you will end up in not unpleasant places in the spring, before the snow has melted in Ottawa. So there is intense lobbying among MPs to get on these travelling committees.

It always puzzled me why the whips didn't use their talent better. If you get justice committee or fisheries committee, there are MPs with expertise in these areas. It may be specialized expertise, but you say, "This man knows fisheries, I'll put him there." I never saw this happening in Ottawa. I hate to say it, but I think it's a way of keeping backbenchers in one's own party, and the opposition leaders keeping their backbenchers, happy.

I think under the American committee system, if you get somebody who's been on a committee for 10 years, there's a lot of expertise there. I think on the American committees in general there's been a gravitation to areas of some familiarity for the congressman concerned.

Keith Martin, Reform and Canadian Alliance MP, 1993–Present

Committees are supposedly the place for making changes to bills. This is where the public comes in to make passionate, intelligent and effective interventions about public policy. In reality committees are make-work projects for MPs. They do reports. Those reports are done with great expense and flourish. They get a day of media attention, and then they are tossed on a shelf to collect dust with thousands of other reports.

Again, look at the 1996 Royal Commission on Aboriginal Peoples. Sixty million dollars, three years of work in the communities, but now never quoted, not used at all. This is an appalling consequence in light of the terrible tragedies experienced by Aboriginal communities across this country. We also have numerous reports of health committee reports that were never implemented.

The minister, through the Prime Minister's Office, basically tells committees what to do. The committees look at bills but have no meaningful input. Public input goes into reports that are ignored. It is an issue of leadership. A leader needs to stand up and say, "I want to make our Parliament democratic. I'm going to make committees work effectively so they can mould bills to reflect what the public wants. MPs will have a useful job and not be obliged to follow like lemmings what the PMO wants, as they do now."

Bills go to committee essentially in their final form and are rubber-stamped with minor changes. We should be following the example of England, where bills come to committee in draft form so that members of Parliament can craft and mould them based on public input, but we are not seeing that at all. It's a perfect example of how Parliament is used to keep MPs busy and stupid.

The penalties can be harsh for an MP who steps out of line in committee. Sanctions can include the loss of prestige inside the party, travel opportunities and the freedom to speak one's own mind without suffering a career penalty.

Liberal back-bench MP George Baker performed one of these "rebellious" actions against his own party while on a committee in 1998. His crime? His committee report criticized the political mismanagement of the Atlantic fishery by the federal Fisheries Department. Most outsiders believe he was booted from his position as chairman of the House of Commons fisheries committee. This is what he told us.

George Baker, Liberal MP, 1974–2002

I was in the centre of a controversy over a report from the fisheries committee. I was chairman of the committee and we were allowed to hold public hearings about fishing areas in Canada. We interviewed the fishermen rather than the bureaucrats or the so-called experts in the system.

In our report we condemned every government that had been in power since about 1965. We singled out certain years, regardless of the political party in power at the time. We said in the report that they had done an absolutely disastrous job of managing the fisheries.

Practically every stock we had was disappearing. Canada allowed 17 foreign nations to fish off the East Coast, the nose and tail of the Grand Banks and the Flemish Cap. How can you have proper management of the fishery if 17 nations have to sit down and determine quotas? We've lived with this system for years, and it's still in place.

It was a unanimous report from all party members of the committee. And I stand by that report today. We recommended that the limit be extended out to 350 miles of jurisdiction over the ocean floor, basically to kick out all of those foreign nations.

Common sense tells you that if you appear to be out of step with your party, you'll be sanctioned. Some people say that I was removed as chairman of the committee, but I wasn't fired. Committee chairmen were reappointed with each new session of that Parliament. Well, who selects the chairman? Each political party selects the members of the committee, and of course the person in favour with their own political party at the time would get the chairman position.

Now, if I were in a position of power within the Liberal Party, would I have reappointed me as chairman of that committee? Why would I do something stupid like that?

The moment came to recommend new members of the committee, and they were changed. The chairman, my position, was given to someone else.

That's the system.

I started to wonder whether I should expand my analysis of the committee system beyond the MPs themselves. I could only speculate on how those who are ultimately accountable to Parliament — i.e., civil servants and other government officials — might view committees. How do they respond to being questioned by MPs and committee members?

I discovered that the current committee structure places considerable power in the hands of the department officials who attend meetings, take the process seriously and learn the secrets of how the committee process works. I also found that certain "rules of the game" are followed by those who are called to speak in front of a committee.

James Bissett, Former Ambassador to Yugoslavia and Senior Civil Servant
When you're preparing the minister to go before a hearing, you put the best face on. And it's not what the committee hears, it's

what the committee doesn't hear, that's often the most important thing because the government is not going to reveal anything that might in the slightest way be embarrassing. They're
public servants; devoted and obedient servants that they are,
they do what they're told to do.

In the last 20 or 30 years there has been a marked change in
civil-service ethics. I certainly noticed that the primary role was
to protect the government from being in any way criticized. As
a result, many of the facts that are held in the public service are
never revealed. The information doesn't come out because they
can't release it.

Bureaucrats don't withhold information independently.
They're told to withhold information by the ministers. It's not
the bureaucrats that are afraid of the access to information,
they're quite happy to reveal all, and often try to do it in devi-
ous ways. But, generally speaking, it's the culture now of the
public servants to work, not necessarily for Canada, but to work
for the minister. The concept of national interest has been clearly submerged in the interest of the political party in power.
Now, maybe we have to live with that, but it's a sad commentary. I think we all recognize that we've got a Parliament that is
basically impotent and the committee system isn't working.

Paul Touesnard, Federal Civil Servant

Questions are planted all the time in the House of Commons.
The questions that are asked by backbenchers, for example, are
often suggested by the minister's office of those respective
departments. So for part of the Question Period there are questions that are asked by the government that are what you would
call planted questions. The same thing happens in parliamentary committees, where each member of the committee has an
opportunity to ask questions while the witnesses are present.
And so some members of the committee who aren't particularly interested in the issue that's being discussed at that particular time may be open to the possibility of asking a question
that the witnesses will be able to easily answer. The questions
may also serve to strengthen or enhance the minister's particular
view on that program or allow the minister to convey his message.

Alan Ross, Former Senior Assistant Deputy Minister, 1986–1993

The biggest technique you had (as a public servant) is you knew that a parliamentarian had very limited time. They had lots of demands, whether it's the constituency, the various committees they work on or the time for the House, so you just worked hard to consume the time they had in front of the Public Accounts Committee. You made sure you survived those one or two hours or whatever it was, and you knew that if you got through that one day, the problem had gone away. It sounds callous but in fact that's part of managing the whole process.

In one instance the House, through the Public Accounts Committee, was asking us embarrassing questions and pushing us for answers that we didn't have. The only thing we could do was say that we would address the issues, but that was not very satisfactory. So basically what you had to do was string out your time.

Today if civil servants go before an estimates committee or before any committee of the House, they know that they can manage those exposures.

Harry Swain, Deputy Minister of Industry, 1992–1995

A deputy minister is accountable to a number of different folks: to the prime minister who appoints him, to the clerk of the Privy Council, to his minister, to the Treasury Board, to all those parliamentary commissioners for information and official languages. So there are a lot of accountabilities here. But a serious one is to Parliament and its committees. I always took it seriously. I always went prepared, in depth, to answer any question that I thought they might ask.

I have to say I never had to breathe hard, yet the parliamentary committees should have made me breathe hard.

One of my regrets about my time in Ottawa is that I didn't deal with Parliament more frequently and more deeply. I found parliamentary committees disappointing. They would get you up there, ostensibly to talk about something serious, and then they'd divide their time into little 10-minute segments, the first six minutes of which were taken up by the member making a speech for his constituents. And just about the time you'd think they were going to pin you down with some interesting question, it was somebody else's turn. Parliamentary committees in that sense became a bit of a game, a bit of a nuisance. They weren't very substantial, usually.

Paul Touesnard, Federal Civil Servant

You certainly don't want to give the impression that the government doesn't know what it's doing. You don't want to appear misinformed or that you can't answer the committee's questions, or give misleading information. You certainly don't want to do that.

What you try to do is prepare yourself for all the possible questions that some people might ask, not counting those you've planted among the government members. You're usually well prepared for those. You do your research to find out what kind of questions the opposing members or some of the renegade members of the government party might ask. That is a little more challenging.

The political realm (the minister's political staff) will try to scope out what the possible challenging questions might be. And if they have some intelligence, you hope they would pass it on to you so you're not caught by difficult questions which would make the whole department or the minister look bad. But that doesn't usually happen.

And we basically put together a reference book and hope that you can flip quickly to the question that's been asked to provide a reasonable answer. You just hope that you can provide an answer on the spot because if you can't, then you probably have to submit a report later on, which you don't necessarily want to do.

Harry Swain, Deputy Minister of Industry, 1992–1995

Now, the other side of that question is, do deputy ministers prepare to avoid answering questions from parliamentary committees? Yes, to a degree we do, in the sense that a deputy owes a debt of loyalty to the government of the day. Those are the folks that were elected by the people to govern. So if a parliamentary committee member — let's say an opposition member — asks a question, and you can keep your minister out of trouble by giving him a literal answer and not volunteering the next six paragraphs, it's probably wise to do so.

Are there any committees that live up to their role of holding the government to account? The only one I could find was the Public Accounts Committee (PAC).

The PAC bases much of its work on the auditor general's report, which does an after-the-fact critique on the government. The committee then holds hearings and makes recommendations to the House of Commons. The following description comes from a booklet issued by the Office of the Auditor General: "Although the auditor general's reports attract considerable attention when they are released, [the Public Accounts Committee] reviews whether public money was spent for the approved purposes with due regard to efficiency, economy and effectiveness."

Donald Savoie, Author of *Governing from the Centre*

There is one mechanism of accountability that stands out and that's the Public Accounts Committee. It stands out for two reasons. First, the chair of that committee is an Opposition member of Parliament, not a government MP, so it has a degree of independence that other standing committees would not have. Secondly, it has access to a lot of resources. The Office of the Auditor General plays a hand in that committee, so it can draw on a number of resources; it can look at past spending patterns. At the moment it appears to have a free rein to move where it wants to move. So it can play havoc with a lot of government programs.

I think one area where the centre (the PMO) has great difficulty is in exerting power to influence the Public Accounts Committee. Thank God for that. The committee enjoys a certain arm's length kind of relationship mainly because the chair is not a government member of Parliament. It's an Opposition member. Secondly, because the Office of the Auditor General also enjoys a degree of independence that other government agencies would not, allowing it to move in ways that other agencies can't.

John Williams, Reform and Canadian Alliance MP, 1993–Present

Accountability is rather esoteric and difficult to grasp. The public goes about their lives — they've got busy lives, jobs to do and families to raise — and they expect the members of Parliament and their elected people to carry out that responsibility on their behalf. That's what they sent us down here to do, and I hope in my small way that I'm making that contribution.

The Public Accounts Committee is the committee that holds a government to account. Unlike the other committees that deal with policy, Public Accounts focuses strictly on government from a retrospective basis. What went wrong? Why did it go wrong? And what are we going to do to fix it to ensure that the taxpayer doesn't end up being taken to the cleaners? So the Public Accounts Committee focuses on all areas of government.

We work very closely with the auditor general, who publishes a report about three times a year and tables it in the House of Commons. By looking at the auditor general's report, we see the full analysis of the issues, the pros, the cons, the facts, the losses, the waste and the mismanagement. From there we're able to understand the issues in depth.

The Public Accounts Committee asks the deputy minister, assistant deputy ministers and those in the senior management positions to come to the committee of parliamentarians to explain why. Of course no bureaucrat really enjoys receiving an invitation to explain why to the Public Accounts Committee. Just knowing that they can be asked to explain why is in itself some measure of accountability for the civil service — to think that we must act properly and prudently on behalf of Canadians.

We don't have the powers to fine and sanction and fire and so on. But we have derailed careers in the civil service by virtue of the fact that testimony in front of the committee obviously demonstrated that some people were incompetent. The fact that you are asked to appear before the committee is not really something that people relish. I, for one, believe that it's an excellent method of accountability. We're not here to hold hands and say to the deputy minister, "I know that you meant well and I know you're going to go back and do a better job." No, we want to ask the hard-hitting questions, to really put them on the spot. These are senior executive officers of large departments in charge of billions of dollars of taxpayers' money.

Harry Swain, Deputy Minister of Industry, 1992–1995

The Public Accounts Committee was usually a little bit different because the Public Accounts Committee had, in the Office of the Auditor General, a very serious staff who could prepare the most embarrassing possible questions for any deputy minister. That would usually keep you on your toes.

As for serious scrutiny by parliamentarians on other committees, of budget estimates, of policies, of past actions, the quality of your performance over the last year or so, it really is a disappointment. I think parliamentary committees are not, as they presently operate, a serious accountability mechanism. They don't have, in general, a staff that can prepare them with penetrating analyses or questions. Their individual members tend to play the partisan game more heavily, a substandard game.

It is rare to find a parliamentary committee taking a view, for example, on matters of administration or of the quality of program delivery, or of estimates or spending or any of that kind of thing. It was not impossible, but rare.

John Williams, Reform and Canadian Alliance MP, 1993–Present

If MPs don't discharge their duties well on the committee, they're certainly not discharging their responsibilities to their constituents very well. Then it's their responsibility to go back and explain to their constituents why they come to a committee and haven't prepared themselves ahead of time.

The vast majority of MPs, being on the other committees, which are policy committees — health care, defence or foreign affairs — are looking at their issues from a prospective point of view. What should we be doing today for tomorrow? They're not looking back. Every department, if it were to look back, would find as many horror stories in their areas as we find.

Harry Swain, Deputy Minister of Industry, 1992–1995

Are you getting value for money in your parliamentary delegate? Maybe. Let me put it this way. There's nothing in the system that says a parliamentarian cannot be highly effective in holding a department to account. In other parliaments, in other congresses, for example, it's normal for individual members to specialize — to be the real specialist on defence or regional economic expansion — to develop deep knowledge of the field and a close knowledge of the players in the field, too. Then on public occasions, like a parliamentary hearing, they are able to ask very difficult questions. These are the kinds of things that expose the dilemmas of politics and public administration and get the most penetrating kinds of answers.

I wish our parliamentary caucuses and the opposition would specialize more and devote more time and attention to learning the fields that they're supposed to be critics for. I think that parliamentarians miss the boat on this account. It's wide open to them to do a better job. Nothing is standing in their way.

Although the Public Accounts Committee garnered a great deal of respect among most of our interviewees, one young Canadian Alliance MP and former member of the committee told my colleague that the PAC "is a cure for insomnia." But at least one committee was attempting to do what committees are mandated to do: hold the government accountable and try to rectify its mistakes.

Sadly, most of the good work that committees do is reported to the Cabinet, which in turn usually ignores the amendments, reports and suggestions. One wonders how that makes the MPs on the committee feel.

Could it get any worse? You bet. Much worse.

When I began looking at the videotape my colleague Rob Roy put together for another documentary our company was developing on the military and Canada's foreign policy, I was staggered by the commonalities between our interviews. Shuffle the details and his interviewees were telling him the exact same facts about committees that my interviewees were telling me. The interesting twist was that many of the people Rob interviewed had experience with both the American congressional committee process and the Canadian system and could compare and contrast the situations. The results are sobering — even embarrassing — for Canadians.

Major-General (Ret) Lewis MacKenzie told an interesting tale of his experience appearing before committees in Canada and in the United States.

Major-General (Ret) Lewis MacKenzie

When I came out of Sarajevo in August of 1992, it seemed everybody in the Western world, all the leaders, wanted to figure out, "What should we do in Bosnia?" Arrangements were made that I would go and appear in front of the U.S. Congress, the first time a Canadian officer had ever done that.

"What do you think we should do?" And my response in a nutshell was, "Nothing, stay out of it. Don't touch it with a 10-foot pole." Well, because that was the Bush administration's philosophy at the time, I got invited back by the Senate.

"What will be the end of our mission?" And I said, "Your grandchildren." Senator Sam Nunn said to me, "What would you advise President Bush to do?" (George Bush, Sr., that is.) And I said, "Absolutely nothing, Senator. I'm a Canadian." And the senator said, "Well, consider yourself an American for 10 minutes and tell us what you'd say." So I went through a long brouhaha on why America shouldn't get involved in the Bosnian situation, which really endeared me to the Bosnian government. They've hated my guts ever since I said it. But nevertheless, at the end of it I said, "If you do go in, you better start training your grandchildren as peacekeepers."

Then our own parliamentary committee wanted to talk to me about Yugoslavia and peacekeeping in general and the military.

I found it bizarre that when I appeared in front of the U.S. Senate I was told, "Give them your own personal opinion." When I appeared in front of Parliament it was, "Here's the party line." I was told, " Don't stray from this and do not criticize government policy." Well, if I'm not going to criticize government policy, then why the hell do you have to ask me? Because if I'm just going to spout government policy, then it's no use interviewing me. Bizarre.

I went in front of the U.K.'s parliamentary committee and once again was told, "Offer your personal opinion." I actually had dinner with 14 of the NATO ambassadors at Raymond Chrétien's place, when he was the ambassador to NATO. The same thing: "Just give them your personal opinion." But in front of my own parliamentary committee: "Here's the party line."

James Bissett, Former Ambassador to Yugoslavia and Senior Civil Servant

I was surprised that I was asked to go before the parliamentary committee. It certainly wasn't at the request of any of the government members that I was there. I was given 10 minutes and I made a statement. Others who were at the same meeting had given their statements. They all ran over the 10 minutes. When I got to the end of my 10 minutes, the chairman told me that was it. Obviously he didn't like what he was hearing. The people around the table, I think, were shocked and surprised that I was criticizing NATO and bringing these things to the table.

What was also interesting was that the man who had replaced me in Belgrade is an old colleague of mine. He was on his way to Sarajevo on a flight when he was suddenly called back to Ottawa because they wanted him to appear before the same committee to counteract what I had said. He wasn't listed as a witness. After I made my statement the chairman then interjected and said they had a surprise visitor and were going to ask him to come up before the committee and give us his views.

So obviously the government wasn't happy that I was appearing before the committee. I think this is a shame because it seems to me an indication that dissent in opposition is not really welcome. We do live in a country where there's free speech. I'm an example of it. I've had a lot of television coverage and everybody knows I opposed the bombing and I've had a chance to express my views in writing and speaking. But before the parliamentary committee? It wasn't a committee that was interested in hearing a former ambassador's views. It wasn't a committee that seemed really intent on getting at the facts and coping with some of these issues. It was obviously a committee that was nervous about my appearance because I might say something that would embarrass Lloyd Axworthy, the foreign affairs minister, or Art Eggleton, the minister of defence, and the government. So I didn't feel particularly comfortable there.

In contrast, when Washington found out I had these views I was invited by a congressman to come down and express them. I had plenty of time to tell what I thought and they listened carefully and asked questions.

When I left Yugoslavia and retired from the foreign service I went to Moscow, heading an international organization there. One of the first Russian members of the Duma that I went to see because he was involved in refugee issues found out that I had been the former Canadian ambassador in Yugoslavia. He asked, "Would you be willing to come before the foreign affairs committee of the Duma and tell us what you think of what's going on in Yugoslavia?" I said, "I will if you understand that I'm not speaking for the Canadian government and I'm not speaking for the international organization I represent, and there'll be no press or media." He said all that would be arranged.

There were about 60 members of the Duma waiting to hear what I had to say about Yugoslavia. They were knowledgeable. They had a lot of good questions. I spent at least two hours with them. I found that a striking contrast because when I came back to Canada from Yugoslavia, nobody was even slightly interested in debriefing me, and I'm sure I would never have appeared before the parliamentary committee had not one of the members decided I might make a good witness.

John Fraser, Former Speaker of the House of Commons

When the military and the Department of National Defence go in front of a parliamentary committee, it's very important that they give enough facts to the MPs so that they can decide for themselves what ought to be done. Now, the defence officials and the armed services personnel do not have to say what the policy ought to be, but they ought to tell people what the situation is. In my view, both as a lawyer and as a former member of the House of Commons, doing that isn't crossing any forbidden boundary at all. If the presentations to a parliamentary committee are written by spin-doctors to make sure that nobody asks a specific question, or if the submissions are, "Don't worry, everything is just perfect," then you're not telling the members of Parliament what they need to know.

We live in a parliamentary system where the majority rules. Governments have been known, sometimes, not to give resources to committees that are going to ask embarrassing questions.

Ted McWhinney, Liberal MP, 1993–2000

Our committees don't have a great deal of expertise. The majority members of the committee, who represent the government's side, control the calling of witnesses. The opposition — because they don't themselves use their expertise to the fullest — are also really not very helpful in putting forward useful, interesting witnesses who will differ from the government line.

It was not my role as the parliamentary secretary for the Department of Foreign Affairs to produce balance among the witnesses. All I could and did suggest — and I met no resistance when I did this — was to say, "Look, we need more information, here are some interesting people." For example, during the Balkan war I knew we had some Canadian experts in this country who could speak on the issue. Yet we were always relying on the representatives of government-funded non-governmental organizations (NGOs) to speak to our committee. I always had the awful feeling that some of these NGOs may be "singing for their supper" — telling us what they thought we wanted to hear — when they appeared as witnesses.

As an ex-lawyer, the other thing that always puzzled me was, why didn't the opposition raise the issue of a lack of expertise by various witnesses who appeared before our committees? If you are lawyer, when you get somebody introduced as an expert you ask, "Well, what's their expertise?" If you go into a court you say, "This is an expert on heart diseases," and if you examine them and find their medical practice has all been in maternity cases, they're dismissed as an expert. I never found any great sophistication in government.

Colin Kenny, Liberal Senator, 1984–Present

I've had a chance to look at how the defence committee functions in the House of Commons and frankly I don't like the amount of control the government exerts over it. It usually has a parliamentary secretary on it who serves as the minister's watchdog, while the chair of the committee tends to get shuffled every year or two. It's not how you have an effective committee.

You need to have chairs that stay on a committee for a period of time, who become knowledgeable and who are prepared to revisit issues regularly. Part of the concern is that parliamentarians haven't been aggressive enough about it and we could certainly improve our surveillance of the military significantly if there was a political will to do so.

I think that it's only when a committee is in place for a period of time that you attract good researchers, and there are an awful lot of folks around who are prepared to provide free advice. There are a lot of retired military folk who know what they're talking about and who are prepared to translate it into language that politicians can understand. It wouldn't take me 10 minutes to find half a dozen who would come forward on different subjects and provide good professional advice.

When we went out and travelled across the country with the Special Joint Committee on Defence, we attracted people in every city we went to. We held hearings in every province and attracted, on one hand, people who were in favour of having no military at all and, on the other hand, people who were in favour of having a vastly larger military. We structured the hearings in such a way that we created a debate that the media were interested in. Frankly, having a defence committee sitting in Ottawa holding hearings simply doesn't catch the attention of the media. You have to go out to the people and then you get the media coverage and the debate develops.

Patrick Boyer, Progressive Conservative MP, 1984–1993

The Americans talk about "oversight," meaning that they're going to examine everything that's going on, to supervise and monitor it. In Canada, and in our English usage on this side of the border, if you say "oversight", that means you overlook it, you miss it: you didn't see it happening right in front of your face, you fool.

The role of our parliamentary committees, whether it is justice, defence or foreign affairs, is to deal with contemporary issues that come up — and have some focused hearings on them. It is to look at the spending practices and the policies of that department, and also to be the watchdog who actually sees what's going on, on the ground, and to hold the government accountable for it. It's a functioning part of a self-governing country.

Unfortunately we often find that the role of parliamentary committees is simply off the radar screen as far as the prime minister and those around him in the PMO are concerned. Unfortunately we have oversight in the Canadian, not the American, sense of the word.

Colin Kenny, Liberal Senator, 1984–Present

The Senate banking committee is arguably one of the most powerful and influential that we have on Parliament Hill. We had the same chair in place there for about a decade. After you've been around for a decade looking at issues, bureaucrats don't fool you so easily, politicians don't scare you anymore, and you have an opportunity to go back and to revisit issues and to be quite effective.

Once a committee's been functioning for five or six years, I don't think you'll hear the deputy minister of finance saying, "Gee, it's too bad that those dummies on the Senate banking committee don't know what they're doing." They know what they're doing. That could be said for defence, if you had people with an interest who were consistently on the committee and putting the same effort into it. I don't think the people on the banking committee are any smarter than the people on the defence committee. They've just been around longer, they have an institutional memory, they focus on the issues and they don't let go. If they get fooled once, they make sure they're not fooled the second time when the same witness comes back. Having the capacity to revisit issues is very important for a legislature, and that's one way that the executive is brought to account.

Ted McWhinney, Liberal MP, 1993–2000

A strength in the United States is the ability to summon witnesses. I've been a witness, and American committees have sought my testimony. Their range is very wide, and they at least read what's being written and say, "We need something to balance our viewpoint, let's have it." But here in Canada I found very little sophistication, in the opposition, in bringing forward witnesses who might have a different viewpoint. This is why in some respects one would like to have maverick MPs around, those who don't follow their party lines. Svend Robinson was not always popular in his own party, but sometimes he did ask the unexpected questions. With the Bloc, I found that they were well-educated, thoughtful people, and they were very helpful in committees, but foreign affairs doesn't have too much impact on traditional Quebec sovereignty issues. It does occasionally, if we get into the issue of recognition, but on the issue of the Balkans, is there a Bloc Québécois position or not?

So the committees, I think, pale in comparison to American committees, and the work that gets done in the United States on legislation just isn't done in any comparable way here. I have friends in the United States who are U.S. senators, and they'd much rather be a senator than a Cabinet minister. The only two posts in the United States that rank ahead of being the senator of a big state would be secretary of state and possibly secretary of the treasury. But there's no job more pleasant than being a United States senator, and frankly, if you organize yourself in your six-year term, you are very fully informed.

As an MP I dealt directly with a lot of United States senators and congressmen. They were very well informed, very well disciplined, and if they themselves didn't have background in an area, they had the staff. And so did the committees. Opposition members, or Republicans if they were the minority party, would have their own council, their own staff. The quality of the questions is very much better, the handling of the issues is better, the policy maker is much more effective.

Major-General (Ret) Lewis MacKenzie

The congressmen and the senators that I dealt with were very knowledgeable. They could take any general on in the American forces, one on one, and talk geopolitics and strategy. In Canada when we have debates on serious issues, whether it's conversion from a UN to NATO mandate in Bosnia, the Gulf War, or Kosovo, each party nominates a representative to read a prepared statement in the House for the record. I've even seen parliamentarians confuse UN and NATO in the same sentence. It's so disappointing to see the lack of sophistication in the capability of the military, what it contributes to foreign policy. To be honest, foreign policy has to be locked in stone before you start talking defence policy, and that hasn't been clearly defined for a long time either.

Even when I go and contribute to a particular report as a witness, and I read their report and say, "That's great. You know, we got our message across," nothing happens. I've given up hope.

Is it any wonder that MPs, too, have lost hope for the committee system in Canada? No matter which way we turned there was increasing frustration that this ever-important institution for MPs has fallen and is continuing to fall by the wayside.

The one prospect that holds a ray of light for change is that most MPs recognize that the committee system is the most likely avenue by which they can achieve power vis-à-vis the prime minister and the Cabinet. Members of Parliament do want to have a say in the bigger issues that shape our country, but the current situation makes them feel impotent. If they can make the committees work better and curtail the party discipline that is ever-present in the system, maybe, just maybe …

In the Speech from the Throne that opened the 37th Parliament in January 2001, the government announced, "In this new session of Parliament the government will make further proposals to improve procedures in the House and Senate …" The next day Jean Chrétien stated in his response to the Throne Speech, "Of course improvements can always be made, but there should be no doubt that Canada's Parliament serves our country very well. Like any human institution, the House of Commons is not perfect. It can be strengthened. Over the years many changes have been made to improve Parliament and more will be made to bring Parliament into the 21st century." And with those words almost every member of his Liberal back bench was optimistic that things would change.

George Baker, Liberal MP, 1974–2002

Look what the Speech from the Throne said. It said that the procedures of the House would be re-examined. Why? Because individual members of Parliament should be able to have more say and more power. I think that probably what that should mean, and the way it should have been stated, and what will evolve, is that the member of Parliament and the backbencher will be able to hold the government accountable for its actions, no matter what those actions are.

Dennis Mills, Liberal MP, 1988–Present

The prime minister has come full circle on this issue, and at his first press conference after the election he said that he challenged members of Parliament to be more creative, show more initiative, and he has carried that forward in not only the Speech from the Throne, but in the speech today in the House of Commons.

So what happened to all that promise over the year that followed? Has the way Parliament works been revolutionized? Do committees now call the government to account, or do they still cheer it on?

Most of changes that occurred came out of the Special Committee on the Modernization and Improvement of the Procedures of the House of Commons (the modernization committee). Here's what two members had to say about their work on the committee, from their contrasting political perches. Committee member Bill Blaikie was interviewed just before the report was released in June 2001, and Don Boudria, the vice-chair, was interviewed just after.

Bill Blaikie, New Democratic MP, 1979–Present

I was involved in a special committee of the House comprising the House leaders, called the modernization committee. But the very name, I think, points to the fact that the government is more interested in process and efficiency and less in the redistribution of power in Parliament. So I don't really expect that what will come out of that committee will address the heart of the matter.

I am confident that the modernization committee, which operates by unanimous consent, will make some valuable recommendations. My only caveat is that I don't think it will be able to address those substantial issues of redistribution of power. I just don't think that that's where the government is at because people who have power like to keep it. That's what stands in the way of all kinds of reform. It stands in the way of economic reform, social reform and parliamentary reform.

183

Very seldom do you see people with a particular kind of power over other people willingly give it up. That kind of power could disappear tomorrow if the Liberal back bench or the government back bench were willing to take chances and live courageously. But that's not happening.

Don Boudria,
Liberal MP, 1984–Present; Current Government House Leader

The changes proposed by the modernization committee will make Parliament work better. They will make government more accountable. We're proposing to increase the funding to the research branch of the Library of Parliament. They're the ones who put together the research papers and other documentation necessary for members to do their work in that regard. Also, when the House is going to use time allocation or closure or measures like that in the future, there will be a mini-debate on it before a vote: does the government really need to use time allocation? We're also going to have another television room. On Parliament Hill there is one room for committees to be fully televised, complete with pre-set televisions for the polling system. And now there are going to be two of those rooms. I think two rooms can accommodate virtually all the committees that want to be televised. I think that's going to be a good investment and it's going to be better.

The system is not flawed. The system is good. The system works well. It needs improvement from time to time. Improvement should be done in a thoughtful way, usually through changes to the rules. It's not universal, but changes should usually be done with the co-operation of all parties in the House of Commons. That's the approach that we use in this report. The report is unanimous.

Bill Blaikie, New Democratic MP, 1979–Present

In the system I want to see, if the majority of members of a committee, including the Liberals, felt after listening to witnesses and testimony that there were problems in a piece of legislation, they could agree to make appropriate changes: "That is a problem, we should fix it." Instead we have a situation where the government says, "No, that is *not* a problem and we will *not* fix it. And it will be passed exactly as is, thank you very much." Committees are charged with examining legislation. They should have the power to amend the legislation and not just sit there, taking orders from the minister. Or for that matter, having the minister take his or her orders from the bureaucracy.

NOTES

1. Quoted in Hutchison, David Gamache, *Executive Backbenches or Political Nobodies? The Role of Parliamentary Secretaries in Canada* (Institute on Governance, November 1999).

CHAPTER 8

Does Your Vote Count?:
The Consequences of a Failing Parliament

In this final chapter we travel full circle back to the first question: Does Your Vote Count? Do Canadian citizens get what they bargain for when they elect their representatives to go to Ottawa on their behalf? And perhaps more dauntingly, can MPs do their constitutional duty under the parliamentary system we operate within? Too few of us are thinking about that important question.

If there is one message here, it is the inescapable importance of having Parliament and our MPs holding the government to account, no matter which side of the political fence they sit on.

Because of the political party system, the power of the prime minister, the utter lack of oversight of how the government spends money and the failings of the committee system, Parliament is not working well. The size of our government has overrun the fading ability of Parliament to control it. The institutional labyrinth has grown so unwieldy that the democratic accountability structures we have in place cannot stop it, correct it or provide a proper vision for the country. There can be no true democratic leadership under such a system.

This is not to say that MPs do not do a good job, per se. They do work hard. They are civic-minded people who by and large care deeply about this country. They are simply operating in a system that doesn't work the way it was designed to. Because they have little influence over the government and cannot hold it accountable, they do their best with what they have. They try to find avenues where they can effect change, but these are mainly on the fringes of what government does. The average MP has little choice but to be railroaded when it comes to the bigger issues. Still, there is the odd victory ...

Judy Wasylycia-Leis, New Democratic MP, 1997–Present

As an opposition member I feel I am playing a useful role, and I think I have more opportunities to stand up and fight for my constituents. I can question the government, I can present ideas at the committee level and I can hold the government to account for its failure to represent people in Winnipeg North Centre. There are frustrations and the pace of change is often very slow, but I know that by being there day after day, raising question after question, I can eventually get through to the government and make a difference. It is challenging and difficult, but also rewarding. I am lucky in many ways and feel it is an enormous privilege to have this position.

We can also express our constituents' will in private members' bills, motions and petitions. The last thing we want is for people to feel so helpless and cynical that they say, what's the point?

I actually succeeded, and it's quite a rare accomplishment, in getting a motion passed by Parliament. I had a private member's motion that calls for warning labels on all alcoholic beverage containers to tell pregnant women not to drink because of the risk of fetal alcohol syndrome. How did I succeed? It came down to having started working on it four years ago. First, I introduced the motion, then I worked with the community groups back in Winnipeg, and thirdly sought support from the other parties in Parliament. Finally, I put out notices and got the community to back this 100 percent. After all that work, in the end MPs felt that it was a good idea and they had to support it. It got almost unanimous support in Parliament. It gives me a sense of accomplishment to have actually effected some change in this place.

The more an issue is presented to the government, the more it gets noticed. When people send letters, faxes and e-mails, government has to pay attention because they are an indication of public opinion. Private members' motions may not have a hope of ever becoming law, but they matter because they can actually inspire the government to steal the ideas and incorporate them into their own legislation. It may be that in the end we do not get credit for the end result, but the important thing is to lay the groundwork behind the scenes and plant the seeds that eventually bear fruit.

Scott Brison, Progressive Conservative MP, 1997–Present

I'll give you an example of how we can effect change. I raised a question on a Friday in the House of Commons directed to the government during Question Period. I asked why the government was posting jobs in the U.S. on its Human Resources Development Canada Web site, a Canadian taxpayer-funded job search site, when they had said that it was doing everything it could to fight the exodus of highly talented and educated Canadians to the U.S., more commonly called the "brain drain."

It was a painfully intuitive, commonsense question, and the response was something to the effect that "the honourable member is wrong. We're clearly not doing that. Why would we do something that silly?" On the following Monday I posed the same question to the government and I was informed by the minister of labour that, in fact, that practice had changed. The government had determined that it wasn't doing it and any such jobs listed (there were 19 on the Friday) had been removed from the Web site.

It was a small but interesting change that illustrates one can make a difference in opposition. If I were a member of the Liberal caucus, then I wouldn't have been given the opportunity as a backbencher to raise that potentially inflammatory issue on the floor of the House of Commons. If I had raised that in a caucus meeting with the Liberals, then I'd be muzzled by the prime minister and they wouldn't do much about it.

So while we don't always get credit on the opposition benches, we can make a difference by contributing to the pressure on the government to respond to the needs facing Canadians. We can make a huge difference by being persistent with a message that is well thought out and consistently well delivered. Even stuck in the far corner of the House, I do get my say.

So while MPs toil on the fringes of the bigger issues facing the country, winning a few here, losing a few there, the larger concern is this: what has the downfall of the MP's clout and of Parliament's scrutiny of government meant to citizens? What about the future of our country and its political system? Many of the interviewees were emphatic about the consequences Canada faces with a weakened Parliament. They also outlined the challenges involved in changing it.

Anne Cools, Liberal Senator, 1984–Present

The citizen is at a very serious disadvantage because the citizen has no mechanism to express opinions. The citizen goes to the polls and votes once every four years, but the citizen is supposed to be represented on the floor of the chamber, through his members. What we're dealing with now is a situation where the magnitude and size of government, with all its resources, is making even asking questions difficult. Members of Parliament don't have the resources and members come and go. It could easily take a new member two or three or four years to begin to know the ropes, much less seek change. In the long run the only correction for this sort of thing is an informed public.

Joe Clark, Progressive Conservative Leader and Former Prime Minister

The institutional capacity of Parliament to control the government is gone, which is not the way the system was designed. That's not healthy for Canada.

We are a very unusual country. The House of Commons is the only national institution that genuinely represents the whole country. Every corner of Canada has a voice here. It's very easy to get a very narrow view in Canada on issues. If Parliament is active, it can force a government to pay attention to a problem in the Northwest Territories or in Cape Breton. That is what Parliament should be doing. When there's too much power with the government and too little with the MPs, Parliament is diminished.

Donald Savoie, Author of *Governing from the Centre*

I think part of the problem here is that we do not let regional concerns surface; instead we just manage crises and don't let troubles surface — there's a big difference. If Atlantic Canada and Western Canada were free to surface their concerns, free to voice some of the criticism, free to explain what doesn't work in their regions, I think we'd have a lot healthier Canada and healthier government. But that's not the way it works. We don't let those concerns surface. We don't see tradeoffs taking place in Parliament, where these concerns ought to be raised.

Keith Martin, Reform and Canadian Alliance MP, 1993–Present

I think Canadians intuitively know something is wrong in the House of Commons, even if they don't know exactly what it is. And that is why we see fewer and fewer people voting. Sixty percent of the public voted in the last election. Only 25 percent — one in four Canadians — actually support the government of the day, and those numbers are declining. So what does that say about our system? It says that our system is becoming more irrelevant to Canadians. I think that is sad because we need this very institution of Parliament to deal with the problems of the nation and to help us achieve the potential that we have in our great country.

Joe Clark, Progressive Conservative Leader and Former Prime Minister

If things continue as they have, the thing most Canadians will do, and in increasing number, is simply drop out of politics. We've seen that in the tumbling voter turnout, particularly among young people. They see no point to the way Parliament now works, and yet we're facing, as a country, decisions that are not only complex but also very difficult. They can't be made unless the people making them have legitimacy and authority. If Parliament isn't trusted and the people who have to make the decisions can't do that with legitimacy, the whole decision-making capacity of the country is undermined.

A change in Parliament matters. There's no question that it matters; however, there's also no question that it's not a top-of-mind issue for most Canadians. Those of us who believe there has to be parliamentary reform have had to argue hard to achieve that, but we have to demonstrate that a Parliament that puts more power in the hands of MPs would also do a better job for the public.

Scott Brison, Progressive Conservative MP, 1997–Present

There are two kinds of ambition. One is ambition to be and the other is ambition to do. For those who are ambitious to do, the House of Commons can be a very frustrating place. My biggest frustration in this place has been recognizing that Parliament, public service in general and electoral office are failing to attract the best and brightest Canadians. To make a real difference, this needs to be a critical mass of some of Canada's best and brightest.

At one time there was a sense of noblesse oblige, when people would make sacrifices and look upon it as a great honour and privilege to serve the public. That has changed.

Ted McWhinney, Liberal MP, 1993–2000

You're not getting interesting, dynamic MPs anymore because there's more competition in going into a multinational company. So that's part of the problem. You're certainly not getting the sort of interesting, bright people that you used to get, say, 30, 40 years ago. It's a very obvious comment.

Can we turn it back? I don't think so. I think the fundamental reforms of Parliament probably really have to go to issue a complete change in the Constitution, separation of powers, American-style and European-style. The country's certainly not yet ready for that. It may occur in the future, but you can see the weakness of the system and the frustrations it brings.

While many of our interviewees were very concerned for the future of the country, a few expressed the belief that Canadians' votes *do* count, and that we get what we deserve in our Parliament. As they see it, when looking to assign blame for the current situation, citizens should look first at themselves.

Gord Lovelace, Former Senate Communications Director

To quote an old adage, "We have seen the enemy and he is us." We deserve the government we have, we deserve the politicians we have and we deserve the political and financial administration we get because that's what we insisted on.

So the fact is that's what politics is. We all think politics is dirty, other than during the six weeks of the election and after the election, when we're going to lose some government program or we want something. Then we revert back to politics.

Canadians want instant political action and we want to see the results tomorrow, so we want our politicians to bring in whatever it takes to do that: policies, legislation, regulation and the accompanying money. On the other hand, the same people who want this also want a bureaucracy, an accounting system — everything tightened right down to the last doorknob — that will administer and keep an eye on every dime.

The fundamental theory is that on one side you have the political, and on the other side you have the bureaucratic and the overseeing which keeps an eye on the political. Your big frustration is you've tried to track down the proof of that and you haven't found it, and it's not surprising you haven't found it.

In politics it's like in so many other things: watch what you wish for because you actually might get it, and that's the difficulty. If we follow through and give power to our representatives, why should we be surprised when they take the fastest but perhaps not the most efficient route to fulfill our wishes?

Stanley Hartt, Former Chief of Staff to Prime Minister Brian Mulroney

Our vote by definition matters only when the prime minister calls an election — that is his business. He does that for his own reasons. By definition citizens' votes only count in elections. Citizens do not go to Parliament and stand outside and vote personally on every issue before Parliament, and they shouldn't. Anybody who thinks that would be a better system hasn't seen a mob before.

The citizen knows all of this. All the citizen has to do is vote strategically, talk to his fellow citizens and say, "Why don't we elect more opposition members? Why don't we have a minority government? Why don't we elect so many opposition members that the government has to stay on its toes and really listen?" But when the citizens say, "We don't like any of the opposition choices. We love the government, to the extent of a vast majority," the citizen is conveying that power to the government. The citizen knows those rules before the citizen votes.

The citizen is making a perfectly valid democratic choice to give those dictatorial powers to the prime minister for four more years. If they don't like what he does, kick him out. I happen to believe it would be healthier if the prime minister got kicked out more frequently but the citizens don't agree with that. The citizens have re-elected the present prime minister three times. The citizens vote knowing the consequence of their vote. They're extensively happy with the result.

Gord Lovelace, Former Senate Communications Director

The good of the country, I always thought, ends at the end of the driveway that belongs to most Canadians. That's just about as far as citizens look in terms of national vision.

When politicians come to Ottawa, they are looking for something that is big at home. Big news back home will get him re-elected and that's not a sad statement at all. I mean, we created a federation so that we could bring our local concerns to Ottawa. It's very simple. Ottawa is a kind of halfway spot between all the hagglers. That is exactly what our politicians are supposed to do: take our little local concerns to Ottawa and try to sell them. I don't think anybody should be ashamed of that.

Has the MP, prodded on by the public back home, demanded all these goodies for his or her riding and in the process stopped being an overseer of the government? Or has the parliamentary system failed, and have the MPs, now with little influence in Ottawa, been reduced to thinking only of the short-term interests of the voters back home, without keeping an eye on which way the government is taking the country?

Either way, the evidence points to a disenfranchisement of the citizen. For if MPs are there to represent us but cannot, then aren't the citizens reduced to nobodies, too? Are there now two nobodies under our system: the MP *and* the citizen?

Anne Cools, **Liberal Senator, 1984–Present**

What worries me, and it is a point that I keep harping on, is that so many sections of our population are now marginalized. There is a state of remoteness between the regions and Ottawa, between the citizens and Ottawa. I'm always trying to do my little bit to bring this information to the public. One of the biggest reasons for these developments in our political condition is because our citizens have become impoverished. Successive governments of this country have impoverished our citizens of the knowledge of how these systems work, and even of the language of Parliament.

Joe Clark, **Progressive Conservative Leader and Former Prime Minister**

The citizen is less part of the equation when the system doesn't work. But the next question is: what do you do about that? Do you try to go to devices that would empower the citizen as an individual? Or do you try to build on the strengths of a parliamentary system? My strong vote is to build on the strengths of a parliamentary system because I think you need to have two things in a society that works. You need to have respect for different individual views, but you also need to have some system by which different views can come together to support a decision. That's what Parliament, in the ideal, can achieve.

Keith Martin, **Reform and Canadian Alliance MP, 1993–Present**

In our country I believe we can pursue excellence because we have the people, we have the resources, and we can make the structures for Canada to achieve the greatness that becomes it.

In our Parliament we have an obsolete system rooted in something hundreds of years ago in a country far away, namely England. Why don't we make a government and a parliamentary system that reflect the needs of our country, a Parliament that is nimble and that can address problems quickly? If we do that, as we must in a fast-changing 21st century, then we will be able to achieve our potential. And if we don't, then we will continue to lag behind other countries, as we are now doing.

We have a situation where our country, with all its riches and potential, could be doing so much better. We are accepting far less than what we should be. I think that is the crux of the matter. Are we satisfied with mediocrity or do we want to pursue excellence?

Anne Cools, **Liberal Senator, 1984–Present**

What is really needed is a reacquaintance between the citizens and government, between the citizens and Parliament. We must simply bring this language and this process close to people. If we say we believe in the citizens, and if we say that we believe in democracy, we simply should give people the tools that they need to follow what is going on. An informed public is a politically charged public and it's a prudent public.

To my mind, the problems of Parliament are not insurmountable. We have a vast body of principles in our background. All that we have to do is to bring them out, shine them up and put them into operation. We would have a far happier system of governance, a far happier Parliament and a far happier electorate.

I do believe this, but maybe I am an idealist.

INDEX